D1325905

Glennyce S. Eckersley is an international angel expert and author of many successful books, including *An Angel at My Shoulder* and *Saved by the Angels*. She lives in Manchester, UK and has made many media appearances.

Gary Quinn is a spiritual teacher, leading intuitive life coach and popular author whose books include *May the Angels Be With You* and *Living in the Spiritual Zone*. He is the founder of Our Living Centre in Los Angeles, California, and is in popular demand for seminars and events, frequently appearing in the media in the States and the UK.

ANGEL AWAKENINGS

*Bring the Angels into Your Life
Each Day of the Year*

GLENNYCE S. ECKERSLEY
& GARY QUINN

LONDON • SYDNEY • AUCKLAND • JOHANNESBERG

1 3 5 7 9 10 8 6 4 2

Copyright © Glennyce S. Eckersley & Gary Quinn 2006

All rights reserved. No part of this publication may be reproduced, stored
in a retrieval system, or transmitted in any form or by any means,
electronic, mechanical, photocopying, recording or otherwise, without the
prior permission of the copyright owner.

Glennyce S. Eckersley and Gary Quinn have asserted their right to be identi-
fied as the authors of this Work in accordance with the Copyright, Designs
and Patents Act 1988.

First published in 2006 by Rider,
an imprint of Ebury Publishing, Random House,
20 Vauxhall Bridge Road, London SW1V 2SA

Random House Australia (Pty) Limited
20 Alfred Street, Milsons Point, Sydney, New South Wales 2061, Australia

Random House New Zealand Limited
18 Poland Road, Glenfield, Auckland 10, New Zealand

Random House South Africa (Pty) Limited
Isle of Houghton, Corner Boundary Road & Carse O'Gowrie
Houghton 2198, South Africa

Random House Publishers India Private Limited
301 World Trade Tower, Hotel Intercontinental Grand Complex
Barakhamba Lane, New Delhi 110 001, India

The Random House Group Limited Reg. No. 954009

Papers used by Rider are natural, recyclable products made from wood grown
in sustainable forests.

Printed and bound in Great Britain by Mackays of Chatham plc, Kent

A CIP catalogue record for this book is available from the British Library

ISBN 10: 1-8460-4061-2 (until Jan '07)
ISBN 13: 978-1-8460-4061-0 (from Jan '07)

Dedicated to all
Spiritual Seekers

Contents

Contents

Introduction

Having worked with angels over the past ten years, we both believe there is a power greater than any of us that guides and helps us in our times of need. It is our sincere desire and hope that *Angel Awakenings* will bring you closer to that power, helping you to explore and deepen your spiritual life, and inviting abundant blessings on your path to a higher consciousness. This book will offer you a daily guide to inspired living, which includes angelic stories, affirmations, blessings, guiding light insights, meditations and exercises. These practices and tools are always available to guide, activate and protect you.

If you read through the book one day at a time, *Angel Awakenings* may even help to give you the focus you need to reawaken your personal sense of divine destiny. 'But how do I start?' we hear you ask. 'How exactly do I focus? How do I figure out what I want in life?' Although ultimately you must work this out for yourself, whenever you need to you can call upon your angels for a little help. And you might also need to find a little time by yourself each day for introspection. Today, life is more frenetic than ever, and time is of the essence, but if you can find just five minutes each morning to read the page for the day, this will bring peace and calmness with which to start your daily routine. Maybe the children need organising for school, or you have a demanding job waiting for you. Retirement may be a challenge, or illness and loss are weighing on your mind. Whatever your needs or difficulties, a few minutes of quiet contemplation as you rise will help you to cope with the rest of your day.

Should you have the opportunity to do so, make a seasonal home altar. Place a coloured candle amid foliage appropriate to the season, add some natural elements such as a stone, a piece of wood, or shells, along with a flower or two. Light the candle, sit comfortably and read the page for the day. Allow yourself time to absorb the words and ask your angel to be with you throughout the coming day.

Give yourself this gift of time: you deserve it, you are a special and unique person, worthy of love and capable of spreading love and peace to all around you. Just a few moments each morning will make a huge difference not only to yourself, but to all you meet during the day. Your inner calm will spread like ripples and enhance the lives of others. The phrase 'little and often' contains much wisdom, for a short time each day to nourish your soul will allow you to grow in wisdom and truly experience angel awakenings.

Be at one with nature, connect to the beauty of the seasons outside your window, give thanks for a new day.

Glennyce Eckersley & Gary Quinn

ANGEL
AWAKENINGS

January 1

For Margaret and her friend, New Year's Day began with great excitement. Hiking with their Church Youth Group in the beautiful English county of Derbyshire, they set out for the hills as the day dawned with a heavy snowfall. Sadly, it soon became apparent that their clothing and shoes were inadequate for such severe weather. As the day progressed the problem became acute, especially when they realised that they had to traverse a frozen waterfall.

Retracing their footsteps was not an option and as Margaret looked down over the steep fall, the village below looked like a tiny toy. Fear gripped her heart as she began to walk across. Her fear was justified because suddenly she felt herself slipping and sliding towards the edge. Immediately, an unknown force grabbed her arm and placed her hand firmly around the ankle of another team member. This, she says without doubt, saved her life.

To this day, Margaret believes her guardian angel held her arm that bitter New Year's Day.

January 2

Outside the open window the morning air is all awash with angels.

RICHARD WILBUR

Guiding Light Insight

We are the personal embodiment of the Divine Nature.

Daily Affirmation

I accept all miracles in my life – now!

January 3

Everything that comes our way represents an opportunity to practise gratitude.

Blessing

May the Angel of Faith protect my heart and mind with light and love.

January 4

'Another year,' sighed Clare, without enthusiasm, 'I can only hope it will be better than the last!' She felt precious little confidence, however, that there would be any improvement – life was about as miserable as could be. The past twelve months had brought the end of a relationship, the knowledge she was surplus to requirements in her job, financial hardship and considerable ill health. Slipping into her dressing-gown, she wandered into her little kitchen with a heavy heart and briefly pondered if there was any point in carrying on.

The morning was bright and sunny, all sparkling frost and deep blue skies, but this lovely sight failed to lift her spirits. Sitting by the kitchen window, she gazed out and began to cry. Sobbing, she told herself, 'So much for the angels; they have abandoned me, it seems.'

A light so intense it put the morning sun to shame instantly filled the little kitchen, and a glow surrounded Clare. Looking up in astonishment but without fear, Clare knew the angels had heard her, and at once was assured her life would indeed change direction. 'I will trust and be positive,' she thought instinctively, 'and transform my life with angelic help!'

January 5

And with the morn those angel faces smile,

Which I have loved long since, and lost awhile.

JOHN HENRY NEWMAN

Guiding Light Insight

We have all been given the power to initiate new ideas and situations, only some of us choose to employ this power while others do not.

Daily Affirmation

I lovingly appreciate myself and others.

January 6

Divine Key

Even if your life appears chaotic, be assured that chaos is often the first step in the transformation to a new awareness and higher consciousness.

Blessing

May the Angel of Light bring me healing, and radiate warmth and clarity in my life.

January 7

William and his friend set out in his little boat for a fishing trip. It was a calm winter's day as they headed out to sea. It was great fun until late in the afternoon, when suddenly the weather became stormy. Mindful of his father's warning not to venture far from the coast, William turned the boat for the shore. But to his dismay the beach was not visible through the driving rain. With a heartiness he did not feel, William assured his friend that there would be a light from the shore to guide them.

At last, a faint light did appear in the distance and so they steered towards it. With huge relief they reached dry land and dragged the boat onto the beach. Calling his father on his mobile phone, William explained their predicament and said they had no idea where they were, but added that they had been guided to shore by a house light. However, as they walked a little further along the headland the boys found a signpost and then William's father knew at once where they were. 'Stay put,' he said. 'I'll soon be with you.'

Driving back the following day to retrieve the boat, William's father asked, 'Where is the house you say guided you ashore with its light?' William realised that there was no house or indeed any other building on that headland. His father laughed and said, only half jokingly, 'You know the guardian angel your mum is always talking about? Well, I guess it was her light that guided you home last night.'

Thoughtfully William nodded; he would not disagree with that.

January 8

The angels ... regard our safety, undertake our defence, direct our ways and exercise a constant solicitude that no evil befalls us.

JOHN CALVIN

Guiding Light Insight

A calm determination to think just what we want to think, regardless of the surrounding conditions, will help us along the highway to a greater realisation of life.

Daily Affirmation

I trust my inner voice.

January 9

Divine Key

Although real boundaries may not limit us, we may
be limited by our false ideas about life and by failing
to recognise that we are dealing with the Infinite.

Blessing

May the Angel of Inspiration radiate uplifting
thoughts and vibrations through all that I do.

January 10

The death of Julie's much loved father came as the last straw in a terrible year. Two earlier bereavements had left her feeling low, but this was unbearable. She had no idea how she would cope with the coming Christmas and New Year celebrations. When the invitation came to join friends on a cruise for the New Year, Julie had very mixed feelings. Could she cope with such jollity at this time? At last she was persuaded to join them and much to her amazement, found herself enjoying the cruise. The fantastic scenery and Caribbean warmth lifted her spirits.

On the final night, she went up on deck alone. Gazing into the beautiful night sky, which was clear and full of wonderful stars, Julie fixed her gaze on one particular star and asked if her father could hear her. And, if so, would he give her a sign? Nothing happened, but she lowered her eyes to the wake of the ship, convinced that the spirit of her father was close. Gazing skyward once more, she gasped, for where only seconds before there had been a completely clear sky, now there was one lone, perfect heart-shaped cloud! Love had indeed found a way.

January 11

And shook his plumes, that heav'nly fragrance filled
The circuit wide. Straight knew him all the bands
Of angels under watch; and to his state
And to his message high in honour rise,
For on some message high they guessed him bound.

JOHN MILTON

Guiding Light Insight

We attract into our lives that which we focus upon
with the strongest intent. The knowledge that good
intent leads to a positive outcome leaves no room for
doubt to grow in the conscious mind.

Daily Affirmation

Today, I am filled with peace and my conscious
mind recognises my complete perfection.

January 12

Divine Key

There is no need to fear the future, for the future will bring you more love, joy and prosperity.

Blessing

May the Angel of Guidance bring me the healing power to transform old habits and beliefs.

January 13

After years of hard work for the same company, Stella thought her loyalty and talents had been undervalued. She realised her heart really lay in working with people. However, where she would find a job in this area was another matter. It all came to a head one night when she was feeling particularly low. Lying on her bed in tears, she said aloud, 'God, please help me.' Suddenly she had the most wonderful sensation of being touched, accompanied by a warm, tingling sensation throughout her whole body. Was this the touch of an angel? she wondered.

Unable to sleep she rose early, deciding to walk to work. As she walked, her spirits rose. Stella could not recall ever walking to work before; it was a long way but today the exercise was definitely beneficial. Turning a corner, Stella bumped into an old school friend whom she had not seen for years and they decided to go for coffee together.

While they were talking, her friend mentioned that she was about to start up a project in their town for underprivileged youngsters. Stella felt her heart leap – how wonderful, she thought. 'We are looking for another leader,' her friend said and added, 'I don't suppose we could persuade you to join us?' Beaming with joy, Stella answered that she certainly would. 'You're an angel,' her friend replied.

'No, I'm not!' laughed Stella. 'But one certainly sent me!'

January 14

The conclusion is always the same: love is the most powerful and still the most unknown energy of the world.

PIERRE TEILHARD DE CHARDIN

Guiding Light Insight

Constant prayer and affirmation are the strongest defences against doubt.

Daily Affirmation

Today, I create peace, truth, beauty, light, wisdom and unlimited good in my life.

January 15

Divine Key

**Learn to live without having to evaluate every
appearance, whilst remaining focused on your desire.**

Blessing

*May the Angel of Love teach me how to love
myself and others.*

January 16

The extended family gathered after the funeral to celebrate the long life of the family matriarch. Happy memories that stretched over a century were shared, with each family member discussing their own particular involvement. For some time, the old lady had expressed a wish for her life to end, saying that she was tired and longed to meet with loved ones who had gone before. Eventually, she had drifted away one evening and her family felt relief and gratitude mingled with grief at her passing.

Here they were, chatting and reminiscing about her on a bright winter's day. Glancing out through the window, one young relative suddenly said, 'Look at the sky!' And there in the centre of an otherwise clear blue sky hung two white clouds in the perfect shape of wings! In an instant they had gone, simply vanishing as quickly as they had appeared. 'She has her wings at last,' the young woman concluded.

January 17

Teacher says a bell rings every time an angel gets her wings.

KAROLYN GRIMES

Guiding Light Insight

Aligning with our inner power is simply a matter of keeping our hearts, our minds and our thoughts focused on the same place: on love.

Daily Affirmation

I am a living, breathing, individualised expression of love.

January 18

Divine Key

Praying for guidance and believing that you have
received it will bring your actions into alignment
with the Divine will and order.

Blessing

*May the Angel of Openness guide my heart
and mind with light and love, and dissolve
all my fears.*

January 19

The house felt huge and empty as Susan wandered from room to room. Gazing through the window at the snow, she tried to picture her son far away in the heat of Australia. The door to her daughter's old bedroom was ajar, and her gaze fell on the crib used by her little grandson whenever he came to stay. It had been six months since the death of her husband and Susan faced the inevitable: she must sell this large house and buy something smaller. That very morning she had an appointment to view a new town house, close to shops and to the bustle of life she badly craved.

The estate agent handed her the key and told her to look around. 'Take your time,' she added. Susan thought that the house seemed just the right size and was in the perfect location. To the rear it opened onto a courtyard, giving a sense of seclusion even in the centre of town. What would her husband have thought, she pondered. Would he approve? Slowly she entered the main bedroom, carpeted in a lovely blue. Susan caught her breath, for there in the middle of the room was a huge, white feather! Yet all the doors and windows were firmly shut against the winter weather.

Stooping, she picked up the feather and softly said, 'Thank you for answering.'

January 20

A blessing on your new home,

A blessing on your new hearth,

A blessing on your new dwelling,
Upon your newly kindled fire.

CELTIC BLESSING

Guiding Light Insight

The ability to stand in acceptance and gratitude is directly attached to our ability to create more goodness, allowing us to live the lives we desire.

Daily Affirmation

Today, I trust my divine presence and move forward to greater accomplishments.

January 21

Divine Key

When you expect to be guided and protected and to receive the benefits of divine will, you can expect the results of all your endeavours to be favourable.

Blessing

May the Angel of Eternal Wisdom bring illumination to everyone and to every event.

January 22

Fiona was enthralled by the sights and sounds of the arts and crafts exhibition, where soon she would be singing with her school choir. Controlling her nerves, she stepped forward for her solo piece and received rapturous applause.

After her performance, Fiona noticed an elderly Chinese lady in one corner of the exhibition hall demonstrating the art of origami. She was also selling beautiful greetings cards made from paper in the shape of flowers. Fiona bought a beautiful pink card with a white floral display that reminded her of an angel. Smiling at Fiona, the lady used a fine brush to paint a message in Chinese on the back of the card in black ink.

Many years passed and Fiona landed a major role in a London musical. For some reason, it had become her custom to take the lovely card with her whenever she performed. As it reminded her so much of an angel, she felt it brought her luck. The first night was a triumph and with cheers from the audience still ringing in her ears, Fiona joined the other cast members for a drink in the dressing-room. One girl, who happened to be of Chinese origin, noticed the card and asked where she had obtained it. Fiona told her, explaining how long she had kept it and that it felt special. 'No wonder,' the girl replied, 'considering what it says.'

'I have no idea what the characters mean,' Fiona told her. With a warm smile, the girl translated for her: 'It says, "One day you will be a star!"'

January 23

It is the song of the angels, sung by earth spirits.

E.W.H. MEYERSTEIN

Guiding Light Insight

There is a law of vibration that accounts for differences between mind and matter; between the physical and the non-physical worlds. From the most ethereal, to the most gross form of matter, everything is in a constant state of vibration.

Daily Affirmation

Today, I welcome greater understanding of life and align myself with compassion and love.

January 24

There is courage at the centre of your being —
courage and peace that can be felt through the day
and into the night. To be courageous is to know that
fear offers no resistance to Love. One of life's
greatest gifts is courage.

Blessing

*May the Angel of the Infinite give me unlimited
power to become a complete individual.*

January 25

The old lady was clearly homeless; she appeared to be carrying her entire worldly goods in two large plastic bags. Unkempt, thin and pale, she slowly walked around the department store. The food hall was packed with wonderful sights and smells, and the old lady looked around longingly. Quickly and unobtrusively, a young man stepped up to the counter and bought a small cooked chicken. In one swift movement he dropped it into the lady's plastic bag. Upon seeing this act, a smartly dressed young woman bought some bread and cheese, dropping these also into the old lady's bag. Confused but thrilled, the old dear gave her a toothless grin then slowly shook her head. Sitting down on a chair she appeared to be in shock. The manager of the food department approached and handed her a large box of biscuits, asking if she had a place to stay that night.

'No,' she replied, 'I sleep mainly in your doorway.' Producing some money, he gave it to her. 'Goodness,' she gasped, 'that will pay the hostel for a week! What a wonderful morning,' she added, 'I can't ever remember having so many good things happening at once.'

The manager smiled and replied, 'That young angel who bought your chicken started a chain reaction!'

January 26

There are angels watching over me and you

Guiding us home, seeing us through

Anytime, any day, anywhere, any way

There are angels watching over you.

MARK HUGHES, FROM HIS WINNING SONG
FOR WORLD ANGEL DAY 2001

Guiding Light Insight

Greatness will come to those who activate their trust
in life. For those who follow that path, each day will
reveal a positive outcome, each moment will yield a
miracle.

Daily Affirmation

*Today, I pray from the heart. I pray for the
highest possible good for all concerned.*

January 27

Divine Key

Since life seems to respond to your beliefs, what if
you were to begin right now to direct your thoughts
and claim your career, receive the healing you desire,
change your situation or alter your reality?
The choice is yours.

Blessing

*May the Angel of Infusion let energy flow
into my life.*

January 28

No one could ever doubt that Rita had a loving family. However, Rita's life was not at all easy and as she was an only child she was left coping with two fragile parents as their primary carer. In her late teens, Rita fell in love with a wonderful young man. This relationship broadened her horizons and life became more light-hearted for her. A year into the relationship she was faced with a dreadful dilemma. The offer of a job in Australia prompted the young man to ask Rita to become his wife and accompany him overseas. With an aching heart Rita realised that she could never leave her parents and so, deeply hurt, the young man went abroad without her.

No word ever came from him and when twenty years had passed Rita found herself completely alone, both parents having passed away. One night before going to sleep, she began to think about the young man, and to wonder how differently life would have been had she gone to Australia with him. She felt no bitterness in her heart, however, knowing that she had made the right decision at the time.

That night, she had a powerful and vivid dream in which an angel took her by the hand and led her through a doorway, where her young man stood smiling at her. All the next day, the dream was with her, it had felt so very real. Then, in the early evening there was a loud knock at her door. With a puzzled frown she went to answer it. There, beaming at her, stood her young man from so long ago!

January 29

There are no accidents; those who are to meet will meet, they are ready for each other.

A COURSE IN MIRACLES

Guiding Light Insight

Awareness of order is active on every level of creation. No being or thing can exist without this process. When there is order, the higher energies flow without hindrance; we feel Trust begging to take over.

Daily Affirmation

Today, I choose to live in my heart energy. I choose to express myself in the true spirit of love.

January 30

Divine Key

Your life is an expression of spirit. You must honour
yourself in total truth and speak only loving thoughts
of yourself and others. You cannot live in the past
or the future – NOW is your moment of truth.
A divine miracle!

Blessing

*May the Angel of Now give me the strength,
understanding and confidence to declare
my Self!*

January 31

Margaret was enjoying her first year in high school. New friends and the new environment filled her with energy and excitement. She especially looked forward to walking to and from school, happily chatting and discussing the day with her classmates.

Walking home one afternoon, Margaret found herself inexplicably crossing the busy road diagonally, without looking. A large, fast-moving double-decker bus slammed on its brakes and swerved violently in an effort to avoid her.

At this point, in the centre of the busy road, Margaret had a sensation of being transported and placed on the pavement opposite without her feet ever touching the ground! Looking back on this incident, she concludes that an angel must have lifted her out of harm's way.

February 1

See, I am sending an angel ahead of you to guard you along the way.

EXODUS 23:20

Guiding light insight

Let us walk with a renewed sense of purpose, accepting each encounter as an opportunity to align with the Divine. When we perceive events as offering opportunities for growth and expansion, our lives will yield extraordinary results.

Daily Affirmation

I am guided every step of the way in my life today.

February 2

Divine Key

If you choose to love you must express yourself
truthfully every day. You cannot hold on to the past
or the future. You must be able to stand in this
moment of truth.

Blessing

May the Angel of Rebirth transform my fears
into courage.

February 3

At four foot eleven inches tall Annie struggled to manipulate her large suitcase on the London Underground escalator. She was distinctly nervous, having been separated by the crowd from her daughter and companion, and now she found herself at the foot of the escalator with her luggage strap caught in the mechanism. Thrust forward by the momentum, Annie fell heavily and was unable to get to her feet because of the sheer numbers of people stepping over her. No effort was made to help her, and whilst her daughter was aware of people crowding on the steps below she had no idea that her mother was in such difficulty.

Eventually arriving almost at the bottom of the escalator, Annie's daughter witnessed a very tall man reach down and lift Annie plus her case in one swift movement and place her out of harm's way. Catching her breath, Annie turned to thank him, but incredibly, within only a second he was nowhere to be seen.

Taking stock, the ladies realised that the man must have been exceptionally tall, over six foot six inches. He had also stood out because he had been wearing a long white trench coat with a hat pulled down over his face, despite the fact that it was a very hot day. He must have had superhuman strength to pick up Annie and her suitcase so swiftly with one arm. And no one had seen him arrive or depart. The trio decided simultaneously that this was in fact a guardian angel visiting Annie when she needed him most.

February 4

For, without being seen, angels are present around us.

St Francis De Sales

Guiding Light Insight

Fear propels us into a cycle of judgement, whilst love allows acceptance and trust. Fear is an ego-based illusion, while love is the ultimate reality of the heart and soul.

Daily affirmation

Today, I walk confidently, trusting life, love and beauty in all areas of my life.

February 5

Divine Key

Life changes daily, so try to keep your attention on what it is that you desire to experience, knowing that today is necessary to create tomorrow's miracle.

Blessing

May the Angel of Good Fortune radiate through my whole being, creating unlimited possibilities in my life.

February 6

Late one night Olga's son was travelling home on the Moscow metro. He was exhausted but very happy to have in his brief-case his institute certificate which proclaimed that he had passed all his examinations with top grades. Dozing for a moment, he woke with a start, realising that he needed to change trains. Leaping up from his seat, he ran to catch his late train. As he breathlessly jumped aboard, he suddenly realised that he had left his case with his precious certificate on the other train! He was distraught: the case had also contained annual results of exams for his entire time at the institute. Beside himself with worry, he called his mother on arriving home.

The following day was a nightmare, as he tried to trace the case in various lost property departments, but to no avail. To make matters worse, the certificate had to be produced before Olga's son could sit the state examinations in three days' time.

To be near her son, Olga stayed in a friend's flat. Suddenly her mobile phone rang: incredibly, the case had been found by one of the teachers from the institute! He had gone through the papers and eventually found Olga's phone number tucked away amongst them. This was the only number anywhere in the belongings. Even more amazingly, the teacher lived close to Olga's borrowed flat. Handing the case over to Olga, the teacher remarked, 'It is such a pleasure to have found this; it would have been so sad to have lost such excellent results.' The angel of syn-chronicity was certainly at work that cold Moscow day.

February 7

Angels mean messengers and ministers.
Their function is to execute the plan of divine
providence,

Even in earthly things.

THOMAS AQUINAS

Guiding Light Insight

The world can distract us from love, but when we
are willing, it can also be a catalyst for showing us
new ways that love is being expressed right where
we are.

Daily Affirmation

Today, I am honest with my feelings and
expressions about myself. I choose an
extraordinary life!

February 8

Divine Key

You too are of the light and the way of spirit, at one
with the Mind that creates all things, at one with the
infinite force within us all.

Blessing

May the Angel of Affluence bring me faith in
myself.

February 9

Even though she had always been fascinated by angels, Sheila was unprepared when she actually saw one. What had otherwise been a wonderful trip to Canada had been marred only by the fact that Sheila had begun to experience headaches soon after arriving there. Never having flown so far before, she thought the headaches might be caused by jet lag. However, the pain became so severe that it had even spread to her gums by the time she returned to England. Her husband drove her straight to see her dentist. Emergency root canal treatment was administered and Sheila was told that this pain was probably caused by infection. However, this diagnosis was far from the end of Sheila's troubles as she suddenly felt extremely nauseous, icy cold and was obviously in shock. So ill did she look that her husband drove her to hospital, where the doctor explained that the dental injection had released some of the infection into her bloodstream.

At long last Sheila was home in her own bed where, with the aid of pills, she slept for twenty-four hours! To her astonishment, on opening her eyes, she saw an extremely pretty lady standing at the foot of the bed. The visitor was holding her head to one side, smiling gently, as if to say, 'Hello, you are awake at last!' A glow surrounded her but she certainly had no wings. She appeared to be flesh and blood, yet, as Sheila stared in fascination, the lady faded and she realised that she had seen her guardian angel. Feeling extremely emotional, she found herself with tears of happiness flowing down her cheeks.

February 10

... like a lily in bloom,

An angel writing in a book of gold ...

LEIGH HUNT

Guiding Light Insight

In times of doubt we should look deep inside; we will find only a miracle waiting to happen. We should celebrate each incredible moment as the gift of life. We are the gift.

Daily Affirmation

Today, I believe in the power of my word and in my ability to experience perfection.

February 11

Divine Key

Love yourself. Forgive yourself for the feelings you may have harboured or still have. This is not about 'managing' or 'mastering' anything. It is about simple healing and self-acceptance.

Blessing

Know that you are loved.

February 12

After many years of hoping 'Mr Right' would appear in her life, Lorna had all but given up hope. But then she met Stuart and it really did feel like love at first sight. A couple of weeks into the relationship, Valentine's Day approached. 'What on earth shall I do?' she thought. 'If I send a card, he might think I am pushy, but if I don't then he might think I don't care!' Eventually, after browsing through the card shops, she found a beautiful card, suitable for any occasion. It was a wonderful photograph of Angel Falls, the world's highest waterfall in Venezuela, South America, and it featured many wonderful rainbows. 'I shall send this and trust the angels to guide me,' Lorna said to herself.

Valentine's Day dawned and lo and behold, a card fell onto Lorna's doormat. Her heart leaped – could this be from Stuart? Excitedly, she opened the card and almost dropped it in amazement. Not only had Stuart sent her a card but it was exactly the same as the one she had sent him: the picture of Angel Falls with all those rainbows! What were the chances of that happening? she thought, and concluded it must be a sign from the angels that she had found her soul mate at last.

February 13

We cannot part with our friends;
we cannot let our angels go.

RALPH WALDO EMERSON

Guiding Light Insight

Compassion does not judge the state of
someone's life. It does not put a valuation on
anyone's life experience. It compels us to recognise
and affirm, through our actions, the truth about
every situation.

Daily Affirmation

Today, I call forth freedom from within my soul;
I release negative beliefs and claim my
Divine Power.

February 14

Divine Key

You don't plant a seed and dig it up a few days later
to see how it is doing! You have implicit faith that the
soil, the seed and the sun are doing exactly what they
are supposed to do. Likewise, when you believe in
your own powerful mind, you will achieve surprising
results!

Blessing

*May the Angel of Transformation move me into
the new dimension of who I truly am.*

February 15

Here is a story of love across the great divide. It is in fact a story about Edna and Joseph (whom we shall meet again, in the month of March). Bereavement is one of the most difficult things to bear in life and, having enjoyed many happy years with Joseph, Edna found life a struggle following his death. The whole family became very concerned when Edna succumbed to a serious illness and had to be admitted to hospital. For a while it seemed that they would lose their mum too.

It was late in the day and Edna was lying peacefully in her hospital bed, one arm resting outside the covers. Suddenly she looked at her family in amazement and told them an unseen hand had taken hold of hers and placed it gently beneath the duvet. Wide awake at the time, Edna knew this was no dream and that no one present had touched her at that moment. However, she recognised the touch of that unseen hand: it was Joseph, once more taking care of her. The encounter certainly promoted her swift recovery in the knowledge that love continues even after death.

February 16

And then he shall send his angels ... and gather together his elect from the four winds, from the uttermost parts of the earth, to the uttermost heaven.

MATTHEW 24:31

Guiding Light Insight

We should learn to accept ourselves and others as we really are at present. When we experience everything completely, both joyous and painful, we cannot help but love. Love is all there is.

Daily Affirmation

Today, I graciously accept miracles in whatever form they may come.

February 17

Divine Key

Know that love is part of your true nature, that love
is part of our true nature and that love tells us all we
ever need to know.

Blessing

*May the Angel of Forgiveness help me to forgive
anyone who has hurt me.*

February 18

Who wouldn't like to spend a relaxing break in Mauritius – what lovely images the name brings to mind. At this time of year, it can be hard to imagine warm seas and sunshine. Alison also had difficulty picturing this lovely place until she stepped from the plane. It was to be the holiday of a lifetime. Having always been fascinated by the beauty and history of this peaceful island, Alison had at last arrived there to live her dream. She was not disappointed and each day she and her travelling companion enjoyed the experience more and more.

One evening, after a particularly enjoyable day, they sat watching the sunset, marvelling at the colours. Feeling relaxed and happy, Alison was jolted suddenly by a voice calling her name. She turned around only to find no one else near. Again she heard the voice and this time she recognised it as her grandmother's! This was simply impossible, but feeling disturbed, Alison decided to call home.

Ringing her mother, she asked if everything was well and explained that, although she was having the most wonderful holiday, she felt uneasy. After a pause to take in the situation, Alison's mother said her grandmother had in fact died a short time ago. 'Believe it or not,' Alison told her mother, 'Grandma just came to say goodbye.'

February 19

It is only with the heart that one can see rightly;
what is essential is invisible to the eye.

Antoine de Saint-Exupéry

Guiding Light Insight

Transformation happens naturally when we surrender to the flow of the Divine energies that give life to
all there is.

Daily Affirmation

Today, and every day of my life, I will see love in
everyone with whom I come into contact.

February 20

Divine Key

The night sky reveals the vastness of the seen
universe. The stars move, the tides pulse, and blood
courses through you. Nothing is permanent, everything changes.

Blessing

May the Angel of Serenity bring a natural flow to
my life and to every circumstance and moment
that life offers.

February 21

This story happened to an acquaintance of our good friend Roy. His friend worked in a sugar beet factory, where his tasks involved boiling the vegetables in order to extract the sugar. High temperatures were involved and so the accident was horrific when it happened. Scalding liquid erupted and covered Roy's friend from head to toe. Even though the ambulance was on the scene quickly there appeared to be little hope that the man would survive. A priest was called, who travelled in the ambulance with him to hospital, trying to calm and reassure him as he administered the last rites. The priest started to pray and at once felt a tingling sensation and a presence join them in the ambulance.

To everyone's amazement, the man recovered and his doctors were astonished at the degree of healing: he did not need skin grafts at all. When he was a good deal better, he sat in bed one day chatting to the priest who had given him the last rites. 'Do you know,' he said, 'and I am sure you will not laugh at me, but when I was in the ambulance travelling to hospital, I saw an angel.'

The angel, he told the priest, had said softly, 'This is not your time.' Again in the hospital, the angel had appeared and repeated the message. 'I knew I would not die!' he told the priest. With a broad grin, the priest told him how he too had felt the presence in the ambulance; he was thrilled to know it had been an angel and to have been part of a modern-day miracle.

February 22

What we know of the blessed above,

But that they sing, and that they love.

WILLIAM WORDSWORTH

Guiding Light Insight

Serenity comes from the soul, that steady centre that nourishes us and helps us understand that the good and bad moments of life do not last, and are but a part of our spiritual growth.

Daily Affirmation

Today, I am creating my perfect life's soul path and I am grateful.

February 23

Divine Key

Love may be romantic, love may be creative, but
most of all love sees itself within all.

Blessing

*May the Angel of Creativity activate my creative
energies within and manifest my own reality of
thoughts, feelings and positive attitudes.*

February 24

There was perhaps just an hour left of light, Martha thought, as she glanced at the clock. It was bitterly cold and she had been calculating how many weeks were left until spring arrived. Tomorrow would be the first anniversary of her husband's death, although it hardly seemed possible that a whole year had passed. The garden looked pretty bleak and she wondered how she would continue to cope with such a large area. Martha decided to ring her son and daughter later that evening to ask their advice about planting. Her husband had loved roses, so perhaps she should plant some new bushes of his favourite colour, yellow.

Predictably, Martha was very tearful the following morning, and didn't know how she would get through the day. Switching on the kettle in her cosy little kitchen, she moved to the large window and pulled up the blind. Her heart missed a beat, for there in the middle of the bare and snow-dusted garden bloomed a single yellow rose!

'Impossible,' she said, aloud. 'How could it be?' The glow in her heart, however, told her that this was the sign she needed to tell her that she would cope. For the rest of her life, the garden would be the place in which she felt closest to her dear husband.

February 25

*All is a miracle, the stupendous order of nature,
the revolution of a hundred million of worlds
around a million of stars, the activity of light, the
light of all animals, all are grand and perpetual
miracles.*

VOLTAIRE

Guiding Light Insight

We build anew when we open our hearts and minds
to the power of the soul and consciously allow the
creative energy to flow through our own divine
beauty.

Daily Affirmation

*Today, I live completely in the present, free
from the worries and fears of yesterday.*

February 26

Divine Key

You too are on the right path, experiencing exactly
what you must experience for your own edification,
regardless of how this may appear to others!

Blessing

May the Angel of Strength allow my greatest

qualities to flow and to create a deep

inner security of peace and happiness.

February 27

Like Martha's tale for 24 February, Lesley's story is about a yellow rose, which is a flower of love and a symbol of heaven associated with St Theresa. For some time Lesley's life had been unhappy. A close relationship had ended for her and her new job was proving to be very difficult. Eventually stress levels forced Lesley to seek medical help and she was instructed to take time away from work. Sadness engulfed her. Tearful and afraid, she thought she might never find the strength and courage to move on with her life.

One night, feeling particularly low, she mercifully fell into a deep sleep. Incredibly, a strong sensation of a presence in the room penetrated her sleep. Waking, she found the room filled with light and a soft, grey figure standing next to her bed. The figure was very tall and powerful in appearance, with wings folded behind his back.

Lesley could hear her heart beginning to beat loudly and she had the strong urge to close her eyes tightly – it was all too much to take in. Closing her eyes for a second, she told herself not to be so shocked: she was blessed by this vision. On opening her eyes again she found the room in complete darkness, the angel gone. In the morning, the events of the night remained clear in her mind and Lesley knew this was no dream, for yellow roses had been placed at the foot of her bed. They were her favourite flower. Lesley was now secure in the knowledge she was being watched over. And, if she could bring herself to trust it, life would be happy once more.

February 28

He gathers the prayers as he stands,
And they change into flowers in his hands.

HENRY WADSWORTH LONGFELLOW

Guiding Light Insight

When we begin to feel exhausted by the conditions
of our lives this may be a call to deepen and expand
our practices of prayer and meditation. And while
this may seem like another demand being placed on
us, when we stop to align with our oneness and
source, the source will provide us with the energy we
need to accomplish anything.

Daily Affirmation

*Today, I accept that there is a reason, season and
time to every purpose.*

February 29

It's a well known fact that moving house is one of the most stressful events in life. If you add to the equation a move abroad, imagine how much higher the stress levels will climb. This was indeed the difficulty that Pam was experiencing. Whilst she was excited to be moving to a lovely foreign location, she was sad to be leaving her family and friends behind and over-whelmed by the practicalities of the move. Following the sale of house and furniture, Pam was left with boxes and boxes of everyday items. Taking advice from enthusiasts she was per-suaded to take these items to a car-boot sale. At break of day one chilly Sunday, she loaded up the car and set off.

To her surprise, Pam was inundated with eager shoppers. Suddenly, the sight of her worldly goods flying off the table seemed so very final that her spirits sank and she found herself thinking, 'Am I doing the right thing?' She became aware of a beautiful little fluffy white feather drifting into her line of vision. It landed directly onto her nose, performed a little somersault like a gentle kiss and floated away into the sunshine. Turning to answer a customer, she was astonished to find it had quite literally disappeared! Pam was bewildered, but concluded this was a sign from the angels not to be afraid.

March 1

Make friends with the angels, who, though invisible, are always with you.

ST FRANCIS DE SALES

Guiding Light Insight

When our conclusions are affirmative, when our wonderings empower us, we are ready to move forward. But what should we do if they are not affirmative? Simply carry on until they are.

Daily Affirmation

Today, I step forward, grateful for all that has passed, knowing that I have the ability to accomplish and achieve all my heart's true desires.

March 2

Divine Key

When you trust the process and allow the Infinite Mind to direct your life, you are being empowered by the most powerful force of the Universe.

Blessing

*May the Angel of Grace manifest miracles
in all areas of my life.*

March 3

The former Yugoslavia was a place much loved by Edna and Joseph. The last time they had stayed at their favourite hotel had been very amusing, for they had arrived to find bright sprinkles of confetti scattered around their room. Having been married for many years they had joked about being in the honeymoon suite. They thoroughly enjoyed their first few days of this trip. However, the end of the week brought tragedy when Joseph suffered a fatal stroke. Edna's heartache was magnified by the sheer confusion of arrangements to be made in a foreign country.

Although grieving herself, Edna's daughter Brenda helped her to cope. One morning at her mother's home, Brenda heard her mother call her in a surprised tone. 'Look what I have just found,' she said, holding out her hand. In her palm were several pieces of brightly coloured confetti! 'I was trying to get this difficult gas fire to light,' her mother explained, 'and on top of the fire I found these pieces of confetti.' Brenda rang the appropriate authorities, who swiftly came to repair the faulty gas fire.

'You are very fortunate indeed,' the repair man said. 'This fire is in a dangerous condition and could have proved fatal without immediate attention.' Brenda and her mother looked at each other, understanding instantly that the confetti had been a warning and that Joseph was looking after his wife and daughter from heaven.

March 4

Sweet souls around us still
Press nearer to our side:
Into our thoughts, into our prayers,
With gentle helpings guide.

HARRIET BEECHER STOWE

Guiding Light Insight

During the times of illness we have faith that we will be healed. During the times of hardship we have faith that our needs will be met and we will not fall into financial destitution. Even when our expectations are not fulfilled we must keep faith, and immerse ourselves in Spirit.

Daily Affirmation

Today, I call upon my divine intelligence to create perfect order in all areas of my life.

March 5

Divine Key

Forgiveness has been thought of and practised as a
way of freeing someone from the emotional bondage
that we have placed upon them. Consider forgiveness as an act of bringing our thoughts into
alignment with all the good of the Universe.

Blessing

*May the Angels of Kindness inspire and care for
your soul.*

March 6

Perhaps the most common symbol of an angel's visit is a feather. So many people tell us that feathers appear in their lives at times when they need reassurance and comfort. Indeed feathers have become known as 'angel calling cards'. We are often asked if feathers have to be white to be significant, but we believe that a variety of colours contain messages. (The colours are listed under the entry for April 5.) Gary's experience is a perfect illustration of this very point.

One morning, Gary was on his way to attend an important meeting to discuss a television project that had been hovering in sight for some time. He was loading his documents into the car when he realised that he had left a file behind. As he returned to get it, he was surprised to see a most unusual brown dove resting in the courtyard of his home, which was situated in a built-up area of Los Angeles not known for bird life. Leaving his home with the file, he happened to glance down and saw a beautiful brown feather at his feet. Bending to pick it up, he thought to himself that it must be a sign. In the event, the meeting proved to be a turning point in this important project, suggesting that the feather had indeed been a sign intended for Gary.

March 7

Around our pillows, golden ladders rise,

And up and down the skies with winged sandals shod,

The angels come and go, the messengers of God!

RICHARD HENRY STODDARD

Guiding Light Insight

Life's passages can become times of celebration the moment we embrace the loving presence, which is always embracing us. Help is not on the way; it is already here, leading us from error to truth, from limitation to freedom, and from good to greater good.

Daily Affirmation

Today, I stand in Truth and Love, perceiving all things as divinely guided.

March 8

Divine Key

We cannot change each other's behaviour. When we
perceive anything other than love, goodness or grace,
it is our own thinking we must challenge, our own
focus we must change, our own self we must forgive.

Blessing

*May the Angel of Honesty give me clarity in
every situation.*

March 9

Carol was delighted to have her daughter Nicola, her son-in-law and their little boy stay with her for a night. Nicola was expecting another baby in the near future. However, later that evening she went into 'serious delivery mode' whilst everyone else went into a panic! Things moved along very swiftly and Carol took charge whilst Nicola's husband tried to dial the hospital, so flustered his fingers simply would not work.

Carol was momentarily overcome with the responsibility and told us that suddenly a line from our book *An Angel Forever* came into her mind: 'Guardian Angel of Wisdom, come to me, please help me now.' Everything happened extremely quickly, but Carol felt peace and calm wash over her. Only five minutes later, Nicola had her lovely new baby safe and sound in her arms. Everyone cried tears of joy and relief.

Minutes later the ambulance crew arrived. Carol had wrapped the baby in a warm blanket and handed the bundle to the ambulance man. 'You have a lovely new son,' she told her daughter. The ambulance man quickly checked the little baby and, turning, said to Carol, 'First thing in the morning make an appointment to see the optician, love!' The baby was in fact a little girl! The evening ended with everyone laughing. Nicola's baby, Teagan Sky, was absolutely fine. Whenever she thinks of that night and holds her precious granddaughter, Carol thanks her angels over and over again for their help in her family's time of need.

March 10

Angels may deliver a message from the realm of Glory,
Or they may work unsung, unseen, in ways we can only begin to think about.

TIMOTHY JONES

Guiding Light Insight

As we begin to discover the truth of our being, even though our awareness may seem small and insignificant, a simple tenacious belief will multiply and expand to fit our every need and desire. This awareness must, by the laws of life, always produce the gifts of good and beauty in our experience.

Daily Affirmation

Today, I am as free as Spirit is free. Every day I am reborn and truly alive!

March 11

Divine Key

The creative intelligence of the universe is forever
bringing change, newness, greater activity and the
opportunity for growth. Your part in this
spiritual/human evolution is to agree to it readily and
participate fully. It becomes easier to say yes to life
when you trust yourself to take another step forward.

Blessing

May the Angel of Purification bathe away the
memory of negativity and doubt, and purify both
my mind and body.

March 12

Sue took a Sunday job in a beautiful little bookshop. However, in spite of her new job, she was in rather a low state and convinced that her life would never improve. The shop owner wasn't present on her first day, and so Sue settled herself in, playing a CD of angel music which filled the shop. Out of the corner of her eye, she spotted Glennyce's book *An Angel at My Shoulder*, which she began to read. Sue found herself wishing that something angelic might happen in her own life and was pleasantly surprised by a lovely breeze across her face.

A customer asked Sue about the details of a painting course advertised in the shop window. Sue explained that she was new and couldn't give her any more information about it. To her surprise, the woman burst into tears. Sitting her down, Sue made her a cup of tea and the lady started to talk. Inexplicably, she had been drawn towards the little shop.

They began to talk about angels, vaguely aware of another woman who was browsing around the shop. Sue pointed out to the lady that the pictures of the angels on display were the work of a local artist, who was also in charge of the art course. At this point the browsing customer piped up, 'I am the artist and would love to have you attend my workshop!' The recently distressed lady beamed with pleasure, and both she and Sue promptly told the artist they would be first to enrol on her course! 'I have no idea why I felt compelled to come to the shop today,' said the artist. Sue gave her new friend a hug. 'The angels,' said Sue, 'arranged help for all three of us that morning.'

March 13

Synchronicities seem to occur when we need them most.

JAMES REDFIELD AND CAROL ADRIENNE

Guiding Light Insight

Our soul has a spiritual resonance, which has been called our magnetic centre. When we hear words of truth, this centre begins to vibrate within us.

Daily Affirmation

I open my heart and my soul to all the opportunities that this new day will bring.

March 14

Divine Key

Your evolution and your survival will become intertwined as you become more willing to change, to
grow and to give up old perspectives and ideas.

Blessing

May the Angel of Release free me from
attachments to the past and from concerns for
the future.

March 15

Two old friends met in the city for lunch. Although they had grown up together, they had both moved away from their childhood haunts. The conversation turned to their shared youth and the people that they both remembered. They laughed together about 'senior moments' as they tried to bring facts and faces to mind.

Walking to the railway station later to catch their respective trains home, they once more tried to recall the name of a music teacher. She had been in charge of the school choir and had a lovely voice. Both women were convinced the name began with D and tried on a few for size, Doreen, Dorothy ... but still the name would not come. Suddenly, as the friends were on the verge of parting, they both remembered the name simultaneously. 'Dawn Bentley!' they cried, consoling themselves that it was in fact forty years since they had seen or heard anything about this lady.

The following morning, a letter fell onto the doormat in one of the friends' houses. Reading the letter she gasped and her mouth fell open. Rushing to the telephone, she called her friend. 'I have just had an invitation to speak at a women's group,' she said. 'And guess who wrote to invite me? Dawn Bentley!'

March 16

Help me to find my happiness in the acceptance of what is my purpose:

In friendly eyes: In work well done, in quietness born of trust

And most of all, in the awareness of your presence in my spirit.

FROM THE BOOK OF CELTIC PRAYER

Guiding Light Insight

Wisdom is found in the heart and soul of every person.

Daily Affirmation

Today, I am dedicated to my application of all my new-found spiritual principles.

March 17

Divine Key

You must open up the blocks to loving yourself.
In order to be free and easy to love, you must open
up that place and let it breathe fresh air, no matter
what the risk.

Blessing

*May the Angel of Peace inspire my human
understanding.*

March 18

Sharon was dissatisfied with her job to the degree that she felt totally trapped by it. She had financial security but was deeply unhappy. One evening Sharon was trying to meditate without success, until finally she threw her hands in the air and asked God to take over the problem. Then she went to bed. Leaving for work the following morning, she spoke to God again, stating boldly, 'By the way, God, I want a clear sign!'

Whilst she waited at red traffic lights, a cycle courier stopped directly in Sharon's path. Circling to face her, he stared at her. The lights changed, but still he would not move. Horns blared behind Sharon and she became bewildered and frustrated. As she watched, the cycle courier began to sign to her, pointing first to his ears, indicating she should listen to him. Moving his hands over the chest area, he indicated, 'Relax and take deep breaths.' Pointing in the direction of Sharon's workplace, he held his nose and Sharon laughed. This definitely meant 'I know the job stinks but breathe and relax!' Then he rode away. As she drove past him, Sharon glanced in her rear mirror, only to find that he had disappeared! Surprisingly, when Sharon related the experience later, a colleague unexpectedly exclaimed, 'That's amazing – clearly a spiritual messenger!'

Shortly afterwards, Sharon's boss created a completely new position for her, eliminating all her previous problems. She now loves her job. Looking back, Sharon believes that God had indeed intervened. What do we think? Well, angels are more than capable of riding bicycles!

March 19

Angels are wonderful and exciting, and they have the appeal of beings who will take care of us and manifest God's personal concern.

ANDREW M. GRENLEY

Guiding Light Insight

A new reality built on new thinking allows us to discover creative aspects of ourselves that we had not previously considered. Experiences of love and gratitude will become more frequent for us. People will begin to spark our interest in new ways.

Daily Affirmation

Today, I am true to all my heartfelt desires and work with passion.

March 20

Divine Key

Decisions not to trust are only constructs of the
mind, and therefore do not exist in any real sense.
One of your jobs in life is to spot the decisions and
beliefs that cause your life to unfold in particular
ways.

Blessing

May the Angel of Freedom send loving energy
throughout my being.

March 21

Like so many of us, Kath occasionally struggles with her computer. Although her computer is essential for many aspects of her job, Kath often finds it frustrating as she is totally new to this area of technology. One morning, whilst she was preparing for an important event, she was thrown into confusion when her computer screen went completely blank. Blind panic ensued as she contemplated the possibility that all her work and preparation had been wiped out.

Kath rang her son Dominic for help. However, Dominic was not at home so she left a message explaining her plight and asked him if he would contact her as soon as possible. Some time ago Kath lost her dearly loved son, Matthew, but she often feels he too is there when she needs help. Walking away from the telephone, she was stopped in her tracks by a familiar voice in her head, giving her instructions for the computer! Having no idea what this message meant, Kath nevertheless went to her computer and pressed the buttons as directed. To her delight, the precious work appeared again on the screen! Quickly, she wrote the instructions down, although she knew she would never forget them.

She wondered what exactly had happened. Was it the voice of Dominic, who somehow had 'plugged in' to her problem before even receiving the telephone message, or was it Matthew helping spiritually? Both, she decided. The boys were working in tandem to help their mum in a time of stress.

March 22

As long as you are asking for help,
You might as well ask for help from the Universe,
You never know what might happen.

ELAINE ST JAMES

Guiding Light Insight

Love is what most of us want. With this in mind, if each of us brings our infinite portion of love into play, no one will go without.

Daily Affirmation

Today, I accept my purpose and manifest love. I know I am love.

March 23

As you move into spring with all its promise and freshness, assess anew what you aspire to in life. Follow this exercise to help you achieve your goals.

Exercise for the Spring Equinox

Do you have any negative thoughts clouding your mind, stopping the good from coming into your life? Remember that angels want to give you what you desire, but can assist you more easily if your thoughts are positive and productive. You must also be responsible for keeping your thoughts and energy in the same positive mind state. Clear your mind and think of any negative thoughts getting in the way of your goal. Then, turn those thoughts around to the positive. For instance, the thought 'I'm not good enough' can become 'I am wonderful and can accomplish anything'. The statement 'I'm not brave enough' can become 'I am the most courageous person ever'. Be bold. And remember, even if you feel fear, continue to trust. This will help you with all your efforts. You are a brave soul, and the angels know it. With your angels as your guides, there is no telling how far you can reach. Use them with love and trust to exceed your wildest dreams.

March 24

Angels appear to us, in whatever guise appears unthreatening and comfortable to us. This certainly appears to have been the case with Patsy; her angel was very unusual indeed, but then so was Patsy's fascination in life. She had, ever since she could remember, been fascinated with the Elizabethan period of history. Books and paintings from the period appealed to her, as did films about it.

All her young life, Patsy had suffered with chest problems and this particular night Patsy was suffering with acute bronchitis. Knowing Patsy's mother to be a qualified nurse, the doctor agreed that Patsy could stay at home, although normally such an ill seven-year-old child would have been admitted to hospital. Sleeping fitfully, Patsy woke in the middle of the night to see a man in Elizabethan costume standing at the bottom of her bed! He looked somehow ephemeral with blond hair and a ruff framing his lovely face. Patsy was convinced she was dreaming but was totally unafraid. Then, she was surprised to find the man was sitting on her bed. This time, Patsy closed her eyes tight and pinched herself before opening them again. Astonishingly he was right beside her. His appearance was more solid now and he stretched out a hand, indicating her chest area, and said, 'I shall take all this away!' He was clearly referring to her chest complaint. Very early the following morning the concerned doctor arrived and was totally astonished to find Patsy completely well. From that day to this, she has had no further chest problems, and is the only member of her family to be so blessed.

March 25

Sleep my child and peace attend thee,

All through the night,

Guardian angels God will send thee

All through the night.

Sir Harold Boulton

Guiding Light Insight

Divinity is everywhere, but it is expressed more in people with pure hearts. Miracles happen for those who are in absolute alignment with truth and compassion.

Daily Affirmation

Today, I love and accept myself just as I am.

March 26

Divine Key

Like the spring, there are the seasons in life as a
whole when we give birth to new ideas or to
children; and we have our own summertime, when
we flourish and celebrate the sunshine and goodness
of our lives.

Blessing

May the Angel of Harmony create balance, love
and spiritual power in every area of my life.

March 27

It had probably been the longest night of Sarah's life. She had experienced not a wink of sleep but had stayed up, brewing endless cups of tea. The morning was stunningly beautiful. Early spring sunshine streamed through the windows and the air was fresh and mild for a day in March. Wandering into the little garden, Sarah wondered if it was too early to ring France, where her much loved little niece and sister lay critically ill following a car accident. Later she would try to book a flight to Paris but first she longed for news of them.

Sarah looked around her fresh spring garden. It felt surreal that all was beautiful and peaceful whilst her heart was in such turmoil. Sitting on her garden bench, she watched the birds for a moment but was suddenly distracted by the sound of music. The music appeared to be getting closer and she had the amazing sensation of being wrapped in this lovely melody. At this point, she was aware that it was not in fact earthly music at all and struggled to describe it when relating the experience. Could this possibly be the music of an angel comforting her? Suddenly her mobile phone rang and she jumped at the intrusion. Swiftly answering she was overjoyed to hear that her family was in fact out of danger. They would probably be well enough to be flown home in a day or so. What a relief, and what a wonderful way to have been helped by the angels at that anxious time!

March 28

And is there enough magic out there in the moonlight to make this dream come true?

BURT LANCASTER IN *FIELD OF DREAMS*

Guiding Light Insight

It is easy to focus our attention on that which we believe makes us different from or, in some ways, even better than other people. Such beliefs are an illusion created from insecurity. In spite of our appearances, at our core we are all the same.

Daily Affirmation

Today, I allow compassion to lead me into the experience of deeper levels of love with all of humanity.

March 29

**We are the true dreamers, and our dreams
accomplish many things.**

Blessing

*May the Angel of Adventure open the way to
experience wholeness by helping me to tune in to
and rely on my inner wisdom.*

March 30

A favourite form of angelic intervention is that of coincidences. Some are more spiritual or life-changing than others. The wonderful thing about coincidences, however, is the more we have faith in them, the more frequent they become. Gary and Glennyce were facilitating a workshop in the beautiful seaside town of Llandudno in north Wales. As lunchtime approached Gary was ending the morning session talking about making our own goals in life and trusting providence. He began to talk about *Charlie and the Chocolate Factory* and how we can all have a winning ticket in life if we trust the angels.

When the session ended, Madeline decided that she would go for a walk in the sunshine. On her return, she was very excited indeed and eager to share her experience. She explained, 'Maybe it was Gary talking about Charlie, but I felt an urge to buy a chocolate bar.' The wrapper blew out of her hand as she opened it, so she chased it and picked it up to drop it in a litter bin. She was amazed to see that the chocolate manufacturer had used the Charlie and the Chocolate Factory story as part of their promotion. The wrapper stated that special bars of chocolate would contain a magic ticket. To her incredulity, Madeline had a winning ticket! To add to her delight, she had won a holiday. Having recently struggled through difficult times, Madeline had felt desperate for a break and that very morning during meditation she had asked the angels for help with this. Here was her answer in a chocolate bar!

March 31

Angels in the early morning,

May be seen the dews among,

Stooping-plucking-smiling-flying,

Do the buds to them belong?

EMILY DICKINSON

Guiding Light Insight

Our dreams are divine thoughts pushing their way
through our consciousness for a greater experience.

Daily Affirmation

*Today, I recognise that I am no longer bound
by limitations.*

April 1

Divine Key

Let us rise above the world of appearances and think
of ourselves as willing participants in the great
drama of constant change – the seasons, the coming
and going of the tides, the birth and the death of the
stars.

Blessing

May the Angel of Positivity bring me thoughts
that nourish and heal.

April 2

It had been a month since Lynn's husband had died and each day was a struggle for her. She longed with all her heart for a sign, no matter how small or simple, just to let her know he was still watching over her. Time passed in a haze until one morning Lynn made a cup of tea, sat down and started to pray. Although this was something she had not done since childhood she felt such a compulsion that day. She prayed intently for help in overcoming her grief and especially that she might receive a sign that John was in good hands and watching her still.

Nothing happened, although she was unsure as to what exactly she had expected. Sadly she returned to the kitchen and made herself another cup of tea. Within seconds, she was totally engulfed in the warm smell of pipe smoke and peppermint. Startled, she glanced all around but there was no one in sight. Chuckling, she instantly recognised that this was her sign: John used to smoke and the instant he had finished his cigarette he would place a strong mint in his mouth. Here she was, surrounded by his personal smell. Tears came again but this time of happiness – she had her sign, and it was indeed heaven scent!

April 3

Numerous are the angels in heaven.

THE KORAN

Guiding Light Insight

**Life itself is filled with infinite possibilities because
we may dream of so much more.**

Daily Affirmation

*Today, I am transformed by the renewal
of my mind.*

April 4

Divine Key

**You are not attached to your history; you are
timeless, an infinite field of creative expression.**

Blessing

*May the Angel of Willingness point me in the
direction of clear wisdom.*

April 5

Feather Interpretations

Feathers are often thought of as angel calling cards, and they can come in many colours.

White: spirituality, purity

Yellow: intelligence, friendship

Green: money, fertility

Blue: psychic awareness

Grey: peace

Red and Brown: healing

Grey and White: hope

Green and Red: finances

Orange: attraction, success

Red: courage

Pink: love

Brown: stability, grounding, health

Brown and White: happiness

Black and White: protection

Blue, White, Black: change

Black and Purple: spirituality

April 6

All night, all day, angels watchin' over me my Lord,

All night, all day, angels watchin' over me.

AFRICAN-AMERICAN HYMN

Guiding Light Insight

Spirit needs to express itself through us, and as we are created by spirit, we can always draw upon the invisible wellspring – that which loves us, knows us and is our source and our supply.

Daily Affirmation

Today, I make a commitment to be true to myself.

April 7

Divine Key

All negative thought-forms can be transformed and re-focused into positive energy.

Blessing

May the Angel of Abundance help me to accept lovingly all people and all situations.

April 8

A group of friends attended a retreat in the Lake District. The spring brought a breathtaking beauty this year. Trees, bluebells, birds and wildlife induced such spiritual feelings that one of the group was inspired to write the following poem.

Reflections at Rydal

As we neared the clearing, / Words and laughter fell away.
In silence we lit candles, / And prepared to close our day.

Lambs and mothers bleated, / The wind sighed through the trees
And leaves passed on the message, / Whispering softly in the
   breeze.

What message were they sharing, / With the softly rippling brook,
Caressing rocks and boulders / On the ancient path it took?

Our chosen words and music / Drifted softly in the air.
Bright songs echoed around us / From birds that gathered there.

As dusk stole through the clearing / And sunlight crept away,
We found the quiet places / Deep inside us – hid away.

And there and then we realised / How connected we all were
To the awesome world around us, / All the beauty gathered there.

And in amongst the music / I thought I heard a sigh.
A gentle soft reminder / That God had just passed by.

DIANE MARSH

April 9

We shall find Peace, we shall hear the angels,
We shall see the sky sparkling with diamonds.

ANTON CHEKHOV

Guiding Light Insight

The willingness to listen to others, and the ability to understand them without judgement, and the broad-mindedness to accept those who disagree with us: these are the signs of true spiritual culture and the awakening of individuals.

Daily Affirmation

Today, I understand my fundamental oneness and activate my pure happiness.

April 10

Divine Key

When we see the entire world as a manifestation of
true consciousness we can align with all people,
plants, trees, animals, mountains and everything.

Blessing

May the Angel of Selflessness open my
willingness to listen to others, to understand and
accept them.

April 11

Probably the most common coloured feather we are likely to encounter is the grey one, due to the proliferation of the common pigeon. That being said, as with so many other signs we receive, it is all in the timing. Helen certainly thinks so: her feather arrived out of the blue and was very timely indeed. The whole world felt grey as Helen woke one Monday morning. It was to be her last week at work, having been told the work force was to be drastically reduced and that her employers 'would have to let her go'. Only recently, Helen had bought a little house and ironically she had a mortgage for the first time in her adult life. Helen felt tears sting her eyes and she wondered how on earth she would survive the day.

That Monday was as grim as she had predicted and it was a relief to close her front door on the world in the evening. Walking into her kitchen, she was taken aback by the sight of a large, grey feather, sitting in the centre of her table! The doors and windows were still firmly shut as she had left them that morning and no one else had been into the house. On lifting the feather, Helen felt a warm glow spread though her – it was like being wrapped in a blanket of peace. We assured Helen that that this was the meaning of a grey feather. She beamed because since that time, not only has everything improved dramatically, but she has been able to remain calm and assured about the whole situation.

April 12

All things bright and beautiful,

All creatures great and small,

All things wise and wonderful,

The Lord God made them all.

MRS CECIL FRANCES ALEXANDER

Guiding Light Insight

The Universe supports its idea of itself in every way. We each have something within us necessary for the evolution of humanity. When we catch what that vision is, everything will conspire to support its manifestation.

Daily Affirmation

Today, I stand grounded in my perfection of God; I release all regret and shame.

April 13

Divine Key

Look in your life and recall something that at the
time seemed impossible to do but through surrender
and compliance, you realised a new idea of yourself.
Friends, family, and strangers showed up offering
love, energy, and motivation, helping you across the
threshold to manifestation.

Blessing

*May the Angel of Surrender help me to let go of
all my self-imposed sadness and attachments.*

April 14

Signs, symbols and messages appear in many forms and the world of nature is often a source of comfort. Butterflies frequently appear at times when a message is needed most. These creatures have always been symbolic of transformation and immortality, often appearing when we are missing a loved one most. Anna was aware of a beautiful Red Admiral butterfly in her garden the day after her sister died. Knowing how much her sister had loved these creatures, Anna took comfort from its presence. The following days passed in a sad blur for Anna and her family. However, to Anna's surprise, not only did the butterfly stay in the garden, but it came nearer and nearer to the house each day.

Rising early the day after the funeral, Anna walked in her garden, where the butterfly was still settled on a bush. 'Well,' she said, 'I am beginning to think Jane sent you to tell me that she is now with the angels. Thank you for your comforting presence.' Later that day, Anna noticed the butterfly had gone, never to be seen again.

April 15

There was a pause – just long enough for an angel to pass, flying slowly.

RONALD FIRBANK

Guiding Light Insight

To flow with the infinite good is to establish ourselves in partnership with the divine. When we are aware that our life springs from the one infinite resource we need never be afraid of the final result.

Daily Affirmation

Today, I stand grounded in my perfection.

April 16

Divine Key

Know that you have everything within you that you
need to manifest your purpose and vision. This may
not be revealed at once, but whatever you require in
order to take the next step is available in the present
moment.

Blessing

May the Angel of Co-operation create healing in
all areas of my life.

April 17

Birds have always enjoyed a freedom denied to humans by their physical restrictions. From the earliest times they have been associated with messages from higher powers. Louise had always found feathers to be of special significance in her life but when her much loved father died, she feels it was a bird that held a message for her.

Shortly after the death of her father, Louise looked out into the garden to see a beautiful, large blackbird sitting on the fence. Its feathers were shining in the sunshine. However, there was one feature of this bird that Louise had never seen before. On the bird's chest was one large white feather. The bird appeared to stare directly at Louise as she noticed this and then, as she watched intently, he plucked the white feather from his breast, flew to the windowsill in front of Louise and dropped the feather onto it, directly in front of her! It was a moment of sheer magic and symbolism, never to be forgotten.

April 18

Morning has broken
Like the first morning,
Blackbird has spoken
Like the first bird.
Praise for the singing!
Praise for the morning!
Praise for them springing,
Fresh from the word!

ELEANOR FARJEON

Guiding Light Insight

Trust that everything you need to manifest love,
abundance and peace in your life will appear.

Daily Affirmation

Today, I trust that I have everything
I need in life.

April 19

Divine Key

Walk through this day assured that every experience
is exactly and perfectly designed for your highest
good.

Blessing

May the Angel of Blessings bring prosperity
and love to my soul.

April 20

The story on 17 April about the amazing blackbird has a sequel, equally dramatic. Only twelve months after the death of her father, Louise lost her mother. It had taken the past year to adjust to the loss of her father and now Louise would have to accept the fact that her mother was gone too. It was a difficult day when Louise and her family attended the funeral but she was sustained by the comforting thought that her parents were now together.

Arriving home later in the day, Louise heard her husband call to her from the garden saying, 'Come and look at this!' Puzzled as to what she would find, Louise went out into the garden to join him. She caught her breath on reaching the garden gazebo because the ground was filled with white feathers. Most heart-warming of all, however, was the fact that sitting in isolation on the gazebo bench were two large white intertwined feathers! 'No mistaking the message this time,' Louise said.

April 21

Our spirits soar on wings of angels.

SARA MICHELLE

Guiding Light Insight

**The intention and fulfilment of our dreams bless and
benefit all with their absolute love.**

Daily Affirmation

Today I am magnificently motivated.

April 22

Divine Key

Today ask your angels to direct your path in what you may perceive as difficult life choices, trusting that love and healing will be the eventual outcome.

Blessing

May the Angel of Power give me the purpose and capacity I need to make decisions for the good of everyone.

April 23

Elaine was a born actress. She never became successful professionally but was a star locally in her amateur dramatic association. As a child she had loved to dress up and now as a wife and mother she would make her little boy laugh, trying on her stage costumes for him. She was a larger than life character and all who knew her were devastated when she was found to be suffering from terminal cancer in her early thirties. 'Whatever will become of my little boy?' she cried, as her husband, doing his very best to comfort her, assured her he would be well loved. He knew in his heart of hearts, though, he couldn't give the child the care and attention that Elaine had given him.

Shortly after the funeral, Elaine's mother arrived to take the little boy to nursery school. With a heavy heart, she urged him to hurry, as he knelt on the chair looking out onto the garden. Suddenly, he began to laugh. 'What can you see?' his grandmother asked.

'Look at mummy,' he replied. 'She is dressed in a long white dress and is showing me her large wings.' His grandmother realised that her grandson thought his mummy was dressing up again for him. She peeped through the window but despite his cries of 'Look, look', she could see nothing – the vision was just for the little one.

April 24

Thy mother's delight,

Fair angels above,

Will guard thee in love.

JOHANNES BRAHMS

Guiding Light Insight

People who select to follow the true path of least
resistance choose to follow their inner guidance,
wherever that might lead them.

Daily Affirmation

Today, I accept only love in my life.

April 25

Divine Key

We cannot erase the past but we can change our
story about it. We cannot change the fact that we
once behaved in a certain way, but we have a choice
about how we interpret our behaviour now.

Blessing

*May the Angel of Compassion help me to
understand all others with the love that
transforms.*

April 26

Today marks a good time to look forward and reassess your goals. Complete this morning exercise.

Exercise for Personal and Professional Clarity

Sit down by yourself in a quiet place in a favourite room of your house. As you are sitting there, think of the personal goals you want to complete. Run them all through your mind, one by one. Now, state each goal. (Ask the angels for help if you like.) As you go through these statements, start your request with 'I am'. This is a more powerful statement than 'I want' or 'I will'. When you have finished, clear your mind and meditate for a minute. Then think about the professional goals you want to complete. Now, think of every career goal you have had up until this point. List your professional goals in your mind. If you get stuck, take a break, and ask your angels for help.

April 27

It is to those who perceive through symbols, the poets, the artists, and seekers for meaning, that the angel makes himself known.

THEODORA WARD

Guiding Light Insight

While we need to do everything we can to heal physically, we also need to release mentally our negative thoughts and old habits, and seek the gift that is hidden within our experience.

Daily Affirmation

Today, I accept the greater good in my life.

April 28

Divine Key

Any way in which you shift to a premise of abundance and a premise of the infinite is a positive action in your soul's journey.

Blessing

May the Angel of Synthesis bring me unlimited energy and appreciation into my soul.

April 29

Angelic symbols and signs are clearly chosen to resonate with the person receiving them. Sally was a passionate gardener and loved flowers, but even so she was amazed at the message she received one bright spring morning. April was perhaps Sally's favourite month – it filled her with optimism and she loved the first spring flowers after the grey of winter. This year, she felt in need of a boost to the spirits more than ever before, as she was newly single after a painful divorce. The previous evening Sally had meditated and asked the angels to help her through this time of sadness.

It was Saturday and Sally opened the curtains on a rainy morning, but at least she could spend the day at home. Walking down stairs she was brought to a standstill by the sight of a large, yellow daffodil on her hall table! There was simply no rational explanation as to who could have placed it there, so Sally did not even look for one: she knew immediately that this was her angel sign.

April 30

*Angels are a reassurance that the supernatural
and the realm of God are real.*

RICHARD WOODS

Guiding Light Insight

When we choose to love, we are affirming our own
greatness.

Daily Affirmation

Today, I have a magnificent gift to bring to life.

May 1

Divine Key

Decide to be the kind of person who radiates light,
walking through life with an unshakeable inner joy
and confidence.

Blessing

*May the Angel of Simplicity attune my soul with
love, intuition and inner guidance.*

May 2

Many of us will be familiar with biblical references to strangers being angels in disguise. The following story has an unusual twist on this. Usually an angelic stranger will help and then suddenly disappear. However, on this occasion the 'stranger' appeared to have the characteristics of a loved one who had recently passed away.

Shirley was on a shopping trip with her daughter and brand-new grandson. Whilst her daughter went inside a shop, Shirley stayed outside with the pram, where she was approached by an elderly gentleman. Peeping at the baby, he fell into conversation with her. As they spoke it seemed that the two of them had much in common, even sharing some heritage details. The elderly man commented on how lovely the little boy was. Shirley thought this was a wild guess as the baby was dressed in white so it was impossible to tell whether he was a boy or a girl. Strangely, all the gentleman's expressions seemed familiar to Shirley and he seemed to know what she was about to say, anticipating her remarks with 'I know'. There was such an air of peace and love surrounding this man that Shirley felt completely at ease.

He walked on and when her daughter returned Shirley related the incident to her, telling her about the comment he had made. The immediate response from her daughter was, 'It sounds like Grandad!' Suddenly all was clear: Shirley believes her father had come to see his new great-grandson, in a guise that would not cause alarm.

May 3

All God's angels come to us disguised.

JAMES RUSSELL LOWELL

Guiding Light Insight

Persistent constructive thought is our greatest tool to
remove the beliefs that cause us distress. It may not
be easy to keep our mental attention focused on an
ideal – but it is possible.

Daily Affirmation

Today, I arise in faith and move forward as a
peacemaker among men and women.

May 4

Divine Key

**This life is short and the universe is patiently waiting
to give you what you most desire. Say YES to life!**

Blessing

*May the Angel of Communication radiate perfect
interaction and synchronicity in my life.*

May 5

It was time for Daniel's check-up with the doctor and his mum Joanna and grandmother Greta were getting ready to take him to the surgery. He was a lovely healthy baby but, as with all new babies, the doctor was keeping a close eye on him. Sitting in the waiting room, the women commented on the fact that they were alone, which was an unusual situation for this busy doctor's surgery.

An elderly lady joined them and was immediately attracted to Daniel. She spoke to him across the waiting room, even though he wouldn't have been able to understand a word she said. As the lady chatted and addressed remarks to the baby, Joanna and Greta found themselves exchanging surprised glances. The expressions that the lady used were unusual and exactly the same as those that Greta's mother, who had died some time earlier, would have used. There was such a familiar air about this lady. Walking across the room, she planted an affectionate kiss on the little boy's cheek. Yet again, perhaps a departed family member was blessing a new baby in a gentle way?

May 6

The angels keep their ancient places,
Turn but a stone and start a wing!

FRANCIS THOMPSON

Guiding Light Insight

The human capacity to reach with our minds and hearts deep into the secrets of the universe, internally and externally, is not just the gift of extraordinary intellects, but it is within the grasp of each of us.

Daily Affirmation

Today, I am deeply grateful and accept complete alignment, love and perfection in my current experience.

May 7

Divine Key

In each moment, no matter what your circumstances are, you have the choice to live in trust or to live in fear.

Blessing

May the Angel of Surrender release the burdens of the past and the negative energies that prevent me from seeing my unlimited inner strength.

May 8

In May 2003 Lesley wrote in her diary: 'Had a very weird dream last night: in front of my bed and extending outside my bedroom, was scaffolding. Four people carried a body along this structure. Following this little procession came another person who stopped and held my hands. Feelings of happiness and sadness simultaneously filled me and left me feeling perplexed. All day I had a strange premonition that something was wrong until I eventually received a phone call from my brother to say my auntie had died.'

Lesley had felt very close to her auntie who, even though she was suffering from Alzheimer's disease, was a very special person. That evening, Lesley went for a walk by the river, thinking about her aunt and soon her tears began to flow. Stopping and looking down, there at her feet she saw a beautiful white feather. Her much loved auntie was not far away after all.

May 9

And yet, as angels in some brighter dreams
Call to the soul when man doth sleep,

So some strange thoughts transcend our wonted
themes,

And into glory peep.

HENRY VAUGHN

Guiding Light Insight

The Universe is a reflector. It shows us the energy
we project onto it. If we choose to live in trust, the
vision in which we trust and into which we put
energy is the one that the universe will mirror back
to us.

Daily Affirmation

Today, I align my thoughts with the goodness,
love and perfection of the universe.

May 10

Divine Key

When you think as a powerful being, knowing you are the embodiment of love, you will manifest things immediately.

Blessing

May the Angel of Integrity release a spectrum of colourful energies into all areas of my life.

May 11

The headache was getting worse and Alice decided to lie down for while in her bedroom. After a moment or two, she became aware of a white mist building up and swirling around her. In the middle of this mist, her mother appeared. Alice's mum had died two years earlier and mother and daughter had been very close. Before her death Alice had looked after her mother, who had had difficulty walking due to a severe leg condition. Alice asked her if she was now free from physical pain. The reply was that yes indeed, she was fine. Then the scene in the room changed and Alice had a vision of her mother dancing in fields. 'You see,' she told her daughter, 'I am back to normal!'

'I love you, Mum,' Alice told her and the reply came: 'I know and I love you too.' Moving towards Alice, her mother encircled her in her arms. It was hard for Alice to put the sensations she felt into words – the warmth, glow and the overpowering love that engulfed her as the light in the room turned to a glowing red. After the encounter, Alice has been left with a feeling of love surrounding her and a complete lack of fear about death.

May 12

Dying is just like passing into another dimension.
Nothing changes, love remains the same.

WILLIAM S. THAW

Guiding Light Insight

The purpose of spiritual growth is not just to heal our own lives for the better; it is also to benefit those around us.

Daily Affirmation

Today, I choose that my life will unfold beautifully, letting all things fall into place.

May 13

Divine Key

We are all beings of consciousness; everything that
we are and do begins with thought.

Blessing

May the Angel of Purpose lead me towards
my goal.

May 14

Marie's experience illustrates that literary 'coincidences' are a common form of angel message. In our book *An Angel Forever* we told the story of Marie's elderly mother's angelic experience. Marie and her mother were looking forward to seeing their story in print. Sadly, before this could happen, Marie's mother passed away. Marie sat by her mother's hospital bed in the early hours of the morning and held her hand as she slipped away. Shortly afterwards, a message arrived urging her to rush immediately to another hospital where her husband lay critically ill. Arriving at the second hospital, Marie was in time to hold her husband's hand as he too died.

Arriving home some time later, still in the early hours of the morning, Marie told her family she wished to be alone for a while to try and absorb what had happened. She silently asked the angels for guidance. As she sipped a drink, she heard the post land on the hall mat and, rising, went to collect it. There was a parcel from Glennyce, with a copy of the book she had been waiting for. A warm glow engulfed her. As she placed the book on her lap, it fell open at her mother's story! Marie found the comfort she had asked for on that sad morning – an answer from the angels.

May 15

Angels know no greater happiness than caring for and instructing those who arrive from the world.

EMANUEL SWEDENBORG

Guiding Light Insight

There's a part of us all that knows the gift we receive when choosing to forgive is much greater than any payoff we might receive from holding on to anger.

Daily Affirmation

Today, I let my past experiences go. They have no power over me.

May 16

Divine Key

If you trust that you're supported by the universe,
you will allow and accept energy forces that will
create powerful changes in your life.

Blessing

*May the Angel of Responsibility give me perfect
guidance in the expression of all my talents and
spiritual energies.*

May 17

A person needs to have a big heart to become involved in charity work. But, as Nicola told us, that heart often comes close to breaking when faced with the plight of some children. When she first became involved with her chosen charity, Nicola was dreadfully distressed about the plight of the children it worked with and often found herself in tears. Out of the blue, she had a vision that showed her tears falling onto fields as seeds and blooming as beautiful pink flowers.

A year later Nicola moved to Australia, where she attended a Buddhist centre. On opening the meditation handbook, she was astonished to find written there an identical visualisation in which tears of compassion were represented as falling like seeds in fields to bloom and bear harvest. Nicola has no doubt that she is being led from above to do her valuable work.

The morning after writing down Nicola's story, Glennyce picked up her daily paper where she read that Dr Peter Petrov and his research team at Essex University had discovered that molecules seemed to line up like two-dimensional crystal flowers when X rays were bounced off tears – a case of science catching up with spirituality!

May 18

It is as if angels were pushing.

ADOLF GALLAND

Guiding Light Insight

The boundless abundance of the Universe is every-where present.

Daily Affirmation

Today, I choose the consciousness of limitlessness.

Divine Key

Negative thoughts, such as anger and attachment,
will destroy any principles of harmony and balance.
You must all trust that you can touch a higher tran-
scendent truth and give thanks for that experience.

Blessing

*May the Angel of Earth make contact with all
aspects of my true nature.*

May 20

Meditation for a Spring Morning

Allow yourself a few quiet moments this morning to follow this meditation. Sit comfortably and relax.

Picture the centre of your heart as a rosebud with tightly folded petals. Slowly the petals begin to unfold until a tiny angel is revealed in the centre of the flower. This angel will guide you through the day. She grows until she is larger than your house, larger than your district and larger than your town or city. Her love radiates over the whole area and she shares your love with the universe too. Waves of love circle the globe and you know that today will be special for you.

The angel slowly decreases in size until she is once more the size of your city, your house and finally your heart. She enters the centre of the rose and, slowly, the petals close until it is tightly folded once more. The angel will stay with you in the centre of your heart all day.

May 21

Look forward angel, now ...

JOHN MILTON

Guiding Light Insight

If we need to be treated a certain way, we will attract
a personality type that will fulfil those needs.

Daily Affirmation

Today, I know that nothing can inhibit the flow
of genius within me.

May 22

Divine Key

In order to create a better world for all humanity we must start with improving ourselves and our daily lives.

Blessing

May the Angel of Communion let me accept and love all individuals.

May 23

Gary's friend Cynthia tells us she has a very close relationship with the angels. She believes that seven distinct angels guard and guide her through life, with its many everyday problems. One particular morning was proving to be extremely trying for Cynthia. A group of business people she had to deal with caused her a great deal of aggravation and she found herself wondering, 'Where are my angels?' Several phone calls made in an attempt to resolve the issue led nowhere and the situation appeared to be becoming more negative than ever.

Cynthia and her husband decided that they would hold a little meditation to the angels in order to achieve some calm. At the end of the meditation, they knew they had achieved clarity and trust, and immediately felt happier in spirit. Only moments later the phone rang: it was one of the people who had proved to be so difficult earlier that day, now working hard to resolve the situation in a calm manner. Truly a swift reply from the angels.

May 24

When anyone prays, the angels that minister to God and watch over mankind gather round about him and join with him in prayer.

ORIGEN

Guiding Light Insight

If we are to live as fully and happily as possible, we will need to train our minds to think in the most dynamic, wise and active ways possible.

Daily Affirmation

Today, I am my own best friend.

May 25

Divine Key

Relationships are also part of the shared flow of the divine within us. If we are in a non-connected mode, we will feel disconnection, regardless of how many people surround us.

Blessing

May the Angel of Obedience give my divine soul guidance.

May 26

At last the holiday had arrived and Penny packed her suitcase with great excitement. The whole family would be going on holiday to Spain. However, Penny felt sadness cloud her happy mood every time she thought about her Aunt Margaret, who had died four months earlier. This would be the first holiday without her. 'I shall miss her so much,' Penny told her mother and was assured that the whole family would too.

The villa by the sea in Spain did not disappoint. Penny was thrilled with her room, which was beautifully furnished and had superb views. Gazing through the window she thought once more of her aunt and said aloud, 'I wish you were here, Aunt Margaret, to see this lovely place.' She felt a warm sensation of arms encircling her and she was suddenly engulfed in a lovely fragrance, instantly recognisable as the scent Margaret always wore. Delighted, Penny realised that Margaret was in fact as close to her as ever.

May 27

Roses of sunshine,

Violets of dew,

Angels in heaven

Knows I love you

AFRO-AMERICAN SPIRITUAL

Guiding Light Insight

**The reality we create emerges from our core belief
system.**

Daily Affirmation

*Today, I trust that the Universe trusts me
in every moment.*

May 28

Divine Key

The universe does not judge; like an echo, it simply
reflects back to you whatever you send out to it.

Blessing

May the Angel of Wisdom create abundance and
knowledge in my life.

May 29

It had been a very testing time for Debs. Everything had been going wrong, culminating in the loss of her job. An expert in stress management, she nevertheless felt severely tested. She asked for a sign that all would be well. Her first sign came as a surprise when she threw back the bed clothes to find lots of little feathers on her pillow, which was tucked away under several covers. Feeling comfort, she went to bed and fell asleep.

As long as Debs could remember, she had had a strong sense of not being completely alone, that someone or some other-worldly being was 'with her'. During the night something woke her – a soft, fluttering noise. This corresponded to an intense sensation building inside her. Sitting up in bed, she met a sight difficult to describe: a large, butterfly-shaped light, vibrating and radiating love, was visible on her bedroom wall. Debs realised this was the internal feeling she was responding to and her heart was being filled with love. Falling asleep swiftly but waking again later, she was astonished to find the light still there. All blinds and curtains were drawn, excluding the possibility that this was an external light. This time the sensations Debs felt were excitement, love and a deep understanding that everything would be well. She simply knows an angel is with her for life.

May 30

On the bridge of colours seven,
Climbing up once more to heaven,
Opposite the setting sun.
Thus the seer,
With vision clear,
Sees forms appear and disappear,
In the perpetual round of strange,
Mysterious change.

HENRY WADSWORTH LONGFELLOW

Guiding Light Insight

Life is a journey on a path to an unknown destination. Each one of us continues on this journey through our own personal experiences and growth.

Daily Affirmation

Today, I find the good in every person, place and situation.

May 31

Divine Key

Learn to look within and you will find what you are looking for.

Blessing

May the Angel of Clarity guide my
actions safely.

June 1

To illustrate that the angels of synchronicity are at work around the globe, our next story comes from Lancashire in the north of England, where Glennyce had been invited to give a talk about angels to a church group. She was happy to see many familiar faces and especially pleased to see Pam, who arrived with a beam on her face, and whose husband had provided the wonderful photograph for the cover of Glennyce's book *Saved by the Angels*. Glennyce chatted briefly with Pam, who mentioned that the evening before the talk she had received a phone call from a good friend, asking if she could recommend a Reiki practitioner for her daughter. Pam immediately thought sadly of her old friend Dot, knowing she would have been perfect. They had, however, lost touch — one of those inexplicable things that happen from time to time. Dot had moved house and Pam had inadvertently lost the new address.

As people started to settle down for the talk, Glennyce made her way to the front of the room. Suddenly, there was a whoop of delight and Pam rushed towards the door, for who had appeared but her long lost friend Dot! Many hugs and kisses later, Pam said it felt like troops coming home from the war — this time, never to be parted.

June 2

In heaven an angel is nobody in particular.

GEORGE BERNARD SHAW

Guiding Light Insight

The Divine Word blesses people everywhere and establishes peace and harmony throughout the world.

Daily Affirmation

Today, I experience life without limitation or constraint.

June 3

Divine Key

Mistakes are lessons, so put your guilt aside.

Blessing

*May the Angel of Unity create a loving,
supportive and incredible situation for me.*

June 4

As many of us can testify, dreams are often powerful and full of symbolism. One night Jean had a most unusual dream: in it, a large white hawk was directly above her and suddenly it began to shed its feathers. Bending down, Jean collected them. At this point, a dark-skinned young man approached her and she handed him these lovely feathers. He reached out and began to wrap a narrow, bright yellow cloth around her wrist, telling her that this was a very special colour for her. Jean told this young man that yellow was actually her favourite colour, even though she never wore it. He bowed, backed away and Jean awoke. It was such a lucid dream that it stayed with Jean all day.

Jean, who is a t'ai chi teacher, went along to lead her class the following evening. Before starting she chatted happily to her students and told them about her dream. At that moment Lynn, another of her students, arrived. She was glowing, having just returned from a holiday in Egypt. Whilst there she had met an Egyptian friend of Jean's and now she was keen to give Jean news of him. Lynn then produced a parcel for Jean. 'Your friend sent a gift,' she told her. Opening it, Jean's mouth gaped open: it was a long, narrow, yellow scarf!

June 5

Miracles arise from a miraculous state of mind, or a state of miracle readiness.

A COURSE IN MIRACLES

Guiding Light Insight

When we live in trust, detached from the how and the details, we open ourselves up to the reality we seek.

Daily Affirmation

Today, I believe in the power of miracles in my life.

June 6

Divine Key

If you trust abundance, you will find yourself
creating it and allowing it into your life.

Blessing

*May the Angel of Delight manifest light into
every area of my life.*

June 7

Jean features in our next couple of stories this month, which revolve around rainbows. In ancient times, man believed rainbows to be bridges over which newly departed souls reached heaven. Angela, Jean's closest friend, adored rainbows and was once fortunate enough to actually run through one – a sensation which, she said, changed her life. When Angela died, Jean visited her family and it was decided that they would all pile into Jean's little car for a day out. Angela's daughter, Gina, her two children Jade and Kyle, plus three dogs, all set out for Glastonbury. Suddenly, after a shower of rain, they found themselves driving through a rainbow. Colours, light and a strange buzzing feeling filled the little car. The bonnet and mirrors reflected the wonderful colours and Gina, tears streaming down her face, turned to say to the children, 'Nana is here.'

By the time Glastonbury came into sight, they had encountered three rainbows. Filled with wonder and excitement, they made their way to the top of the Tor. Breathtaking beauty unfolded in front of them and Jade asked quietly, 'Do you think Nana is still with us?' It was then that the most beautiful rainbow of all appeared, and everyone agreed that Nana was indeed still with them. It was a day none of them would ever forget.

June 8

Over all our tears, God's rainbow bends
To all our cries, a pitying ear he lends,
Yea to the feeble sounds of man's lament,
How often have his messengers been sent!

CAROLINE NORTON

Guiding Light Insight

We don't have to generate or create love. When we release our need for another person to change in order for us to be happy, the power of spirit rises naturally within us, filling us with its love.

Daily Affirmation

Today, I wish myself and others well.

June 9

Divine Key

Your thoughts and your attempts to be free will keep
you bound whenever you direct your energies to the
outside. This is because the situation is really
created on the inside, in your consciousness.

Blessing

May the Angel of Expectation always allow me to
experience the best of everything.

June 10

You will recall the story on 4 June about Jean and the yellow scarf that was given to her as a gift from her Egyptian friend.

Once, when visiting Egypt, Jean had been travelling on a bus with her friend Khaled. It was so dry and dusty she asked if they ever experienced rainbows in this arid land. Khaled explained that he had only ever seen a rainbow on film or television, and that it only rained one day per year in that area of the country.

Once more Jean began to think about Angela and how she would have loved the adventure of a trip to this fascinating country. Suddenly a traveller on the bus leapt to his feet and shouted something in Arabic. Others followed, shouting excitedly. Turning to her friend, Jean asked what was going on. At this point Khaled too stood up, cheering loudly and speaking to their fellow passengers, at which point all eyes were on Jean. Looking through the window, Jean saw a rainbow! Khaled had told everyone that he and Jean had only just that moment been talking about rainbows and he now explained that the other passengers clearly believed this western woman to be a magician. However, Jean knew that this rainbow meant that Angela was with her once more. Even more extraordinary was the fact that at that moment Radio Cairo filled the bus with Eric Clapton's famous song 'Tears in Heaven', which had been played at Angela's funeral!

June 11

There let the way appear.

Steps unto heaven

All that thou sendest me,

In mercy given.

SARAH F. ADAMS

Guiding Light Insight

Everything that happens to us is attracted to us by
our own thoughts.

Daily Affirmation

Today, I activate my power of choice and choose
the experience of being a rich and joyful person.

June 12

Divine Key

It is very easy to focus on the cost of living and then
to miss the gift of living and the gift of giving.

Blessing

May the Angel of Balance release all my

limitations.

June 13

We have all experienced periods in life when everything appears to be going wrong and we find ourselves thinking whatever will happen next! Amanda had certainly experienced one of those times.

One evening before going to bed, she decided to choose an angel card for inspiration and to read a little from her copy of our book *An Angel Forever*. The following morning, she began to sort through some papers and books, which were piled high on a very heavy wooden shelf in her home office. To her amazement, out of the corner of her eye she saw a lovely white feather directly in the centre of the room, on the carpet. Intrigued, she turned and took a couple of steps into the centre of the room to pick it up. At that precise moment the heavy wooden shelf fell from the wall, missing her head by inches! The heavy books stored there, plus the weight of the wooden shelf, would at the very least have rendered her unconscious. It did prove one thing, however: Amanda says, 'No matter how dark things appear, the angels are still watching over you.'

June 14

I have learned that no matter what happens, or how bad it seems today, life does go on and it will be better tomorrow.

MAYA ANGELOU

Guiding Light Insight

Surrendering to the natural flow of energy and spiritual wisdom will create incredible healing on all levels of life.

Daily Affirmation

Today, it is perfectly right for me to be abundant and happy.

June 15

Take care with that which is seeded in your mind. Keep it fresh, good and loving, or you may be surprised by what you've grown.

Blessing

May the Angel of Travel give me protection, and may I and my companions always journey safely.

June 16

When we first met we were surprised to learn that, as a young woman, Glennyce had spent several years living in the same area of Los Angeles that Gary lives in now. Glennyce had lived there very happily with a family as the nanny to their three little boys. Amanda's story on 13 June reminded Glennyce of an incident that took place all those years ago in California.

The eldest boy, Jonathan, had a shelf above his bed on which was placed a small fish tank containing a couple of goldfish. One night, when Jonathan's parents were away for the weekend, Glennyce had put the boys to bed and fell asleep herself. But during the night, she was awoken by the sound of the telephone. Answering, she heard Jonathan's grandmother say, 'Glennyce, I am so sorry to ring in the early hours of the morning but I cannot sleep for worrying about the fish tank. It is right above Jonathan's head and what will happen if we have an earthquake?' As small quakes did happen all the time in the area, Glennyce assured her she would move it. She placed the tank in another room and returned to bed. Minutes later there was a large earth tremor that shook everything in the house. At the time Glennyce thought it an unusual coincidence, but today she believes the timely call was protection from the angels.

June 17

Hush my dear, be still and slumber,
Holy angels guard thy bed!
Heavenly blessings without number,
Gently falling on thy head.

ISAAC WATTS

Guiding Light Insight

When we feel that we are moving away from positive thoughts and drifting back into doubt we can bring our attention, breath, thoughts and words back to our own truth.

Daily Affirmation

Today, I act in the knowledge that I possess an eternal, infinite and abundant supply of inner and outer riches.

June 18

Divine Key

To experience love for others you must love them
simply because you love them, and that means loving
them unconditionally.

Blessing

*May the Angel of Beauty give me unlimited
radiance.*

June 19

It was lovely to receive a letter from Isabel in Timaru, New Zealand. Isabel had been in touch with us for some time, and she had even given us a wonderful angel story for our book *An Angel Forever*. Amazingly, that book features in Isabel's new tale.

Climbing into bed one night, Isabel felt uncharacteristically out of sorts, although she did not know precisely why. As it was her habit to read for a while before going to sleep, that night she picked up her copy of *An Angel Forever*.

The following morning, Isabel was making her bed and, on throwing back the duvet, she saw to her surprise a perfect, delicate, pure white feather lying on top of the blue under-sheet. It was so beautiful that, Isabel says, 'It lifted my heart.' She found herself saying out loud, 'Where on earth have you come from?' Isabel's bedding did not contain feathers and this particular feather had certainly not been there when she went to bed the night before. Well, she concluded, no matter how it had arrived, one thing was certain – it had brought her the peace of mind she needed at that time and for that she thanks her angels.

June 20

Our destiny, our nature and our home,

Is with infinitude, and only there;

With hope it is, hope that can never die,

Effort, and expectation, and desire,

And something evermore about to be.

WILLIAM WORDSWORTH

Guiding Light Insight

When we come across a group of people who are speaking badly of someone, we will assist in raising the vibration of the planet if we do not join in their criticism.

Daily Affirmation

Today, I accept new thoughts of love, peace and joy, trusting that the best is sure to follow.

June 21

Divine Key

Never fall victim to pessimism. Patience, optimistic faith and enthusiasm are essential in life; and we must always strive to cultivate these qualities and to keep them alive in our hearts.

Blessing

May the Angel of Sanctuary fill me with complete bliss.

June 22

The space between heaven and earth is like a bellows.

The shape changes, but not the form:

The more it moves, the more it yields.

TAO TZU

Meditation

At my spiritual centre I know, by accessing the power of One. I claim my good with perfect assurance that it is right. I speak as the embodiment of wholeness and love. All I require comes to me effortlessly – for I believe in my word. Doubt and fear are left behind and I confidently proceed with my life. I accept this good for myself and everyone. I accept this with gratitude and love.

June 23

We have reached the time of the summer solstice and our motivation for the summer months should be high, with glorious days to raise our spirits. Here is an exercise to mark this important turning point in the year.

Exercise for the Summer Solstice

Create a list of things that you would like to achieve over the next few months. Pick the goal from your list that seems the most challenging and make this goal your focus. Give a word of 'pre-thanks' for achieving this goal, even though you haven't physically mastered it yet. Write it down, exactly as you want it to happen. What does your goal look like to you when you finally achieve it? Is it in a nice location? Does it come to you easily? Are you having fun while you are working towards your goal? Remember, your angels want to give you everything you desire. Free yourself of cares and let pure abundance enter your life.

June 24

Communication with angels starts if you recognise they're there.

MARY STEINMAN

Guiding Light Insight

The Hebrew word *Shalom* is commonly understood to mean 'peace'. What many non-Hebrew-speaking people do not know is that *Shalom* also means 'whole' or 'wholeness'.

Daily Affirmation

Today, I allow my heart to be in harmony with the whole of life.

June 25

Divine Key

Pay close attention to your mental chatter so that you can determine if you are empowering or disempowering yourself.

Blessing

May the Angel of Care fill me with
loving energy.

June 26

Everyone agreed that Ben would be an actor when he grew up. Not only was he quite brilliant at interpreting his part in plays, but he could control his nerves beautifully. At the age of eleven he was rehearsing for the end of term play. It was a long and complicated part for one so young but his teacher had every confidence in him. And Ben did not disappoint.

Later that night, as Ben prepared for bed, his mother told him how proud the family was of him. Being rather shy herself, she found it amazing that he could control his butterflies. 'Grandpa Wilson helps,' came the reply.

As Ben's grandfather had died several years before, his mother was startled and asked, 'How, darling?'

'He always taps me on the shoulder just before I start and I know he will make sure all goes well,' Ben explained. His mother says that his grandpa must be at his shoulder still, because Ben is now a professional actor!

June 27

Who knows the thoughts of a child?

NORA PERRY

Guiding Light Insight

When we outwardly manifest our thoughts we create our reality.

Daily Affirmation

Today, I accept prosperity and perfect alignment with my source of supply.

June 28

Divine Key

When we align with Spirit as our only source and
supply, we will not be thrown off course by any
negative situations. We will simply be reminded to
turn within and align with our divine source of
supply.

Blessing

*May the Angel of Universal Choice fulfil my
greatest expression.*

June 29

On Craig's seventeenth birthday, his grandmother died. As they had lived two hundred miles apart, Craig had seen his grandmother only a couple of times a year and he was sad not to have had a chance to say goodbye to her. Now, driving from his home in Edinburgh to Yorkshire for the funeral, Craig thought how this would be the first time in years that the whole family would be gathered together.

The morning after the funeral Craig and his family went to the little house where she had lived. Walking ahead, Craig reached the house first and was taken aback to see a face peer out at him from the bedroom window. He did not recognise the face at all – it was a pretty young lady with a sweet smile. Maybe someone was staying there, keeping an eye on things, he thought. Knocking on the door, he waited in anticipation. 'No point knocking,' his aunt said. 'The place is empty and I have the key.'

Deciding not to say anything, Craig went straight upstairs to the room that overlooked the street. It was completely empty, but a wonderful scent filled the air. Had he seen an angel peeping down at him, he wondered, perhaps to reassure him that his grandmother was in her care? He decided that this must be the explanation but that he would keep the knowledge to himself, as he felt that it was his personal angel as well as his grandma's.

June 30

He that is slow to anger is better than the mighty; and he that ruleth his spirit than he that taketh a city.

PROVERBS 16:32

Guiding Light Insight

Expose yourself constantly to wealthy ideas: think prosperity, think substance, think affluence.

Daily Affirmation

Today, I allow myself to grow and heal.

July 1

Divine Key

**The opportunity to experience peace in our lives is
offered through the realisation of our wholeness.**

Blessing

*May the Angel of Spontaneity free me from all
limiting beliefs.*

July 2

Whilst staying in a beautiful area of France, Jane loved to take her cousin's dog for a walk. One day, arriving home from a walk, Jane discovered that she had lost one of her favourite gold earrings. It was not only valuable in monetary terms but held great sentimental value, as it was a gift from her husband. For several days, Jane searched for her precious earring, but to no avail. Sadly, she had to accept that it had well and truly gone.

Each day, Jane walked to the top of a steep hill where there was a clearing in which stood a lovely blue cedar tree. Jane found this to be a spiritual place and would often pause there to say a little prayer or meditate for a short time. She did this one morning a week after losing her gold earring. She says that she heard something as she started to walk away. She couldn't explain exactly what it was, but it was not a conventional voice – more a sense of knowing, implying that she would find her lost earring. Jane says she smiled to herself, believing this to be a fanciful notion. But then, just ten paces along the path, she saw her earring lying there, shining in the grass! It was in a spot frequented by walkers, riders, and even off-road vehicles, which made the find seem even more incredible. 'This,' says Jane, 'was my own minor miracle.'

July 3

The more we love what is good and true, the more angels love to be with us.

EMANUEL SWEDENBORG

Guiding Light Insight

There may be very difficult times in our lives, and in those moments the acknowledgement of the highest good for all can be comforting. We must have the faith to align with spirit and accept another new experience without attachment to the outcome.

Daily Affirmation

Today, I believe in and accept miracles
in my life.

July 4

The word yoga means 'union', the joining of all that is other in the One.

Blessing

May the Angel of Union inspire me with compassion and empathy towards all beings.

July 5

No one knew quite how their argument had begun but the fact remained that the two sisters had not spoken to one another for many years. Appeals for reconciliation fell on deaf ears, as Hilda and Edna vowed to have nothing more to do with each other. The situation was further complicated by the fact that Hilda had moved to be nearer her son, which meant that the sisters now lived fifty miles apart.

On the morning of her seventy-fifth birthday Hilda looked out of her window to see a car pulling up at her front door. Astonishingly, her sister Edna climbed out of it. Almost in shock, Hilda opened the door at a loss as to what she might say. However, as her sister approached they simultaneously burst into tears. Apparently, Edna had experienced a powerful dream in which an angel had told her she must visit her sister. When she related this to her daughter, she found herself being made to pack an overnight bag and being bundled into her daughter's car before she changed her mind! It was a marvellous birthday and the sisters promised to stay in touch.

Only a week later, Hilda was diagnosed with a terminal illness and both sisters realised that the angel had appeared just in time.

July 6

From the unreal lead us to the real,

From death lead us to immortality,

From darkness lead us to light.

Guiding Light Insight

A loving relationship with a conscious partner creates a space wherein we can remember our wholeness.

Daily Affirmation

Today, I am honest and loving in my relationships.

July 7

Divine Key

The past is done; this is a new moment and a new
day. It's time to trust yourself.

Blessing

*May the Angel of Birth bring newness
into my life.*

July 8

It had been a dreadful week and the agony just seemed to keep on coming. Struggling to deal with the end of a relationship and trying to cope with the news that her brother had been diagnosed with cancer, Martine did not know where to turn. The one person she longed to speak to was her father, as he would have known exactly what to say and how to comfort her. There was little point in wishing for that, however, as Martine's father had died two years earlier.

Wandering into the kitchen to make a drink, Martine was astonished to find the largest butterfly she had ever seen in her life. Not only was it huge but it was brown and white in colour, a combination she had never seen before. Feeling comforted by this sight she went to bed.

For a whole week, the butterfly rested on her kitchen shelf and Martine could only marvel at the beautiful creature. Her feelings of despair lessened and one morning she found herself saying aloud, 'Dad, I will cope with this and I know you are watching over me.' The butterfly immediately fluttered from the shelf out through the open window!

July 9

Seek not to change the world, but choose to change
your mind about the world.

A COURSE IN MIRACLES

Guiding Light Insight

When we trust that we possess the recipe for success
within ourselves and the willpower to create it, we
will find ourselves achieving the success we desire.

Daily Affirmation

*Today, I step out of my comfort zone and enjoy
incredible new experiences.*

July 10

Divine Key

To live a life that is filled with peace and ease, you first need to trust the essence from which you create your very self. You are trustworthy. When you come to know that, all other extensions of trust begin to open up. The choice is always yours.

Blessing

May the Angel of Patience bring success to me.

July 11

Problems or pain often feel so much worse at night. When we wake alone in the early hours it can seem as if the whole world is happily asleep whilst we suffer in silence. Certainly this was how Maureen felt. Recently bereaved, she found it difficult to sleep and the fact that she really did not have any close family made her predicament worse. 'If I have an angel,' she thought, 'I don't know where she is at the moment.' She got up and went downstairs into her kitchen to make a cup of tea. As she walked by the telephone in the hall, to her amazement she saw that there was a message on the answerphone. It seemed very odd, as she had been at home all the previous day and could not recall the telephone ringing.

Listening to the message, she found tears streaming down her face: the message was from a good friend she had not seen since the funeral of her husband two weeks previously. The recording told Maureen that she and two other friends would be arriving that morning at 10 a.m. to take her out for the day. They had been thinking about her and wanted her to know how much they loved her. 'My angel was here after all!' Maureen exclaimed aloud.

July 12

Angels descending bring from above
Echoes of mercy, whispers of love.

FANNY J. CROSBY

Guiding Light Insight

When we notice that we are drifting into fear, lack
and limitation, we have a choice about whether we
direct our minds back to healthy, positive thoughts.
The challenge is to hold onto positive thoughts
clearly and consistently.

Daily Affirmation

Today, I am vibrantly alive.

July 13

Divine Key

Our fear is that if we forgive, our walls of protection
will crumble, leaving us vulnerable. The truth is, we
are always vulnerable.

Blessing

*May the Angel of Healing radiate energies of love
and cleansing through me.*

July 14

We met Nicola earlier in this book, on 17 May, and here is another lovely story of hers that we would like to share with you. It involves dolphins. Now, it is a well known fact that dolphins appear to have an affinity with humans and many people who swim with them say the experience is quite magical. This appears to be especially true if the person is suffering in some way, whether physically, mentally or emotionally.

Nicola was on a visit to New Zealand, where she had enjoyed a lovely holiday but now found herself laid low with a virus that was hard to shake off. In spite of feeling a little off-colour, she jumped at the chance to swim with the dolphins. She was soon splashing about with a lovely creature called Kelly and found she loved the experience. Looking up from the pool, she saw lots of white feathers floating down towards her and settling on the water! Nicola laughed and initially dismissed the feathers as being caused by seagulls, which was the most obvious explanation, but she realised that the timing was particularly significant. Lots of spiritual coincidences have surrounded Nicola these past two years and she feels sure the angels are guiding her.

July 15

And after these things I saw another angel come down from heaven, having great power; and the earth was lightened with his glory.

REVELATION 18:1

Guiding Light Insight

We must open ourselves to invite a feeling of unity to come upon us. Once we have rejoiced in that whole-ness, our next mission is to reach out and include others in oneness.

Daily Affirmation

Today, I know that support is always available to me.

July 16

Divine Key

When it is yourself you need to forgive, a large,
looming creature usually stands in the way: Guilt.
Guilt is accompanied by a false sense of responsibility for someone else.

Blessing

*May the Angel of Tenderness touch
and heal me.*

July 17

Earlier in this book, we quoted a verse from Mark Hughes's winning song that he performed at a World Angel Day. Diana Cooper had rung Mark only days before the event to tell him he had won the competition and to ask him to sing it live on the day. Even though Mark had written a beautiful song about angels, he was totally unaware of any symbolism or signs that might indicate an angelic presence in his life. However, that would soon change.

On the Friday morning before the Sunday event, Mark left for work as usual. Incredibly he found up to a hundred white feathers sprinkled over the roof of his car, parked in the drive! Mark says that it was as if two pure white doves had been fighting on top of it. It's true to say that it was a lovely still morning, but when Mark arrived at work he was nevertheless amazed to note that none of the feathers had blown off the car roof. His surprise was even greater on the Sunday morning when he heard Diana talk about the significance of white feathers – he told us that you literally could have knocked him down with one!

July 18

The secret of creation lay in music
A voice to light gave being.
Sound led the stars to their places.

LYDIA MARIA CHILD

Guiding Light Insight

Humility allows us to remember the times we may
have said, 'I would never …' and then, days, months
or years later, we have found ourselves doing exactly
what we swore we would never do. It gives us permission to acknowledge the ways in which we may
have caused pain or sorrow for other people.

Daily Affirmation

Today, I recognise the gift of infinite life in me,
as me.

July 19

Divine Key

Humility and realism are the entryways to the forgiveness of others and also entryways to forgiving yourself.

Blessing

May the Angel of Perfection bring me balanced relationships with everyone.

July 20

Ellen put on her favourite floral dress and when the hairdresser had fashioned her white hair into soft waves, she declared herself ready. Leaning on her walking-stick and the nurse's arm, Ellen stepped from her room and went along the corridor to the large bright lounge of the Residential Home. As she approached the door, the singing of 'Happy Birthday' filled the air and applause broke out. The room was festooned with balloons and a banner that read: 100 today! Beaming, Ellen made her way to her favourite chair which was placed by the large window and which was covered in birthday cards. No sooner had she opened her cards, than the door burst open and a crowd of children, grandchildren and great-grandchildren appeared. They were laughing noisily and carrying a huge cake, bunches of flowers and bottles of champagne.

It was a most exciting of mornings culminating in the arrival of a reporter from the local paper. Chatting for some time, he then asked Ellen the inevitable question: what was the secret of her longevity? Her reply was a little surprising. 'Well,' Ellen said, 'on the eve of my birthday I always thank the angels for taking care of me during the past year and ask if they will let me have another one. And so far they have granted me one hundred!'

July 21

For he shall give his angels charge over thee,

To keep thee in all thy ways.

They shall bear thee up in their hands,

Lest thou dash thy foot against a stone.

PSALMS 91:11-12

Guiding Light Insight

Love can be viewed as the very active energy that connects all beings, whether they are consciously aware of this connection or not.

Daily Affirmation

Today, I enjoy asking for and receiving exactly whatever I need and desire.

July 22

Divine Key

The more you acknowledge grace, and say 'thank you' for moments of grace, the more grace will appear in your life.

Blessing

May the Angel of Consciousness bring me guidance and synchronicity.

July 23

Building a large sandcastle is virtually obligatory for families on holiday and the Martin family took to the task with vigour. The children ran to the sea with their buckets to fill the huge moat. However, the happy scene suddenly turned to panic as Anna realised her daughter Lucy had not returned from the water's edge. The family ran up and down the beach, shouting for Lucy, their hearts racing with fear.

Some ten minutes passed when suddenly a shout went up: 'There she is!' Sure enough, sitting on top of a large rock was Lucy, wearing a bemused look on her face. Dashing over to her, her father lifted her down. The entire family hugged her and wondered how on earth she had managed to climb such a large rock. Indeed, no one else nearby appeared to have seen her climb it.

When they returned to the hotel, Anna asked Lucy how she had got up there. 'I was in the water,' Lucy said, 'and the waves became big, but the beautiful lady picked me up and put me on the rock.'

'What did the lady say?' asked her mum.

'Nothing,' replied Lucy. 'She just smiled!'

Anna and her husband exchanged knowing glances. 'You always said the children had guardian angels,' Anna's husband said, 'but I didn't expect them to be on the beach!'

July 24

For an angel of peace, a faithful guide,

A guardian of our souls and bodies, let us entreat
the Lord.

LITURGY OF THE EASTERN ORTHODOX CHURCH

Guiding Light Insight

Everywhere we look in the universe we see prosperity, as life recreates itself abundantly and magnificently. Prosperity is the experience of love, success, peace, abundance, freedom and the joy we have always wanted.

Daily Affirmation

Today, I welcome help and security into my life.

July 25

Divine Key

Know that everything in your life will work out for
the highest good. Be aware of your thoughts and
only speak positive ones. Love yourself, your body,
and your whole being.

Blessing

*May the Angel of Flexibility create openness
for my spirit to flow.*

July 26

Although Umbria was lovely Mary and John still had a strong desire to see Rome while they were in Italy. A daytrip there meant catching a train at 6 a.m., but the effort proved worthwhile as it was an amazing day. The heat and the walking made them both tired, so Mary and John ordered a cooling drink in a café. At this point it dawned on them that they had no idea how to get back to the train station. Feeling rather vulnerable, they were cheered up by a young lady who joined them and started to chat. They told her of their predicament and how the only sight they hadn't seen was the Spanish Steps.

The lady was quite beautiful, with blue eyes and blonde hair. She guided them to the Spanish Steps, and then she took them to a bus stop where she explained which bus would take them quickly to the station in time for their train. Relief flooded through Mary and John as they thanked her. Next to the bus stop Mary spotted a beautiful dress shop, where she and the lady looked into the window. Perhaps a second passed before Mary turned her head to say something, only to discover that her companion had completely disappeared. It was impossible for her to vanish in just a split second, Mary thought. Then she remembered that the lady had told them that she too had never been to Rome before! There was only one conclusion: they had met a guardian angel.

July 27

This is indeed what the divine voice, the thunder,
echoes 'Da – da – da: restrain yourselves, give, be
compassionate.'

BRHADARANYAKA UPANISHAD

Guiding Light Insight

All life can be seen as love. This is truly the essence
of what we are in the world.

Daily Affirmation

Today, I allow my light to shine brightly.

July 28

Divine Key

Trust that you are the best and choose to surround
yourself with only successful people. Make choices
that move you into your greatness!

Blessing

*May the Angel of Partnership help me to share
abilities and talents with everyone.*

July 29

One beautiful July evening two close friends took their seats for a performance by the Welsh National Opera company. This was a special occasion for many reasons. The two friends had recently lost their husbands, John and Lewis. Both men had loved music and in particular opera; in fact, Lewis had been a professional musician. This evening in the beautiful surroundings of Llandudno was to be the friends' personal memorial tribute for their husbands.

When the interval came Padma and Barbara took their drinks outside to look out to sea. The sky was completely clear and a deep blue, but as they gazed at the ocean, something remarkable happened. There in the centre of the clear blue sky, two rainbows appeared. Not the conventional arched rainbows, but two vertical columns of rainbow colours! Barbara, a science graduate, declared that it was impossible, but she said to Padma, 'It's as if Lewis and John have joined us in spirit.'

Nodding her agreement, Padma replied, 'It feels as if their auras are filling the sky!' One thing was certain, however: both friends felt that their loved ones were very close indeed.

July 30

The Universe is always singing,
And man must learn to listen,

So that his heart may join the universal chorus.

Sarah Martha Baker

Guiding Light Insight

Living fully means something different to everyone.
Each person's choices for their life are very different
from those of the next. This weaving together of experiences makes life the colourful tapestry that it is.

Daily Affirmation

Today, I write an illuminated script for my life,

knowing spiritual perception guides my choices

and governs my decisions.

July 31

Divine Key

The gifts of life are to be found everywhere, every day – not just on holidays. Decide you are a gift to all life, and act upon that decision. Once you know, accept and affirm yourself as a gift to all, your presence will act as a catalyst for attracting divine healing, love and joy.

Blessing

May the Angel of Sharing shower me with sacred blessings.

August 1

A pool party sounded terrific fun and Nina could scarcely wait. Her best friend was going to be twelve and her friend's parents had hired the local pool for her birthday party. Although Nina was not a good swimmer and would normally not have been quite so keen to go swimming, this was different, as all her friends would be there and they would have a great time.

Most of the afternoon had been organised with pool games and at last it was time for food. Everyone left the pool quickly and Nina found herself rather isolated in deeper water than she was comfortable with. She struggled to reach the poolside, but became rather tired and didn't seem to be getting anywhere. In a panic, she tried to scream for help and, swallowing water, started to sink. Thrashing around she felt very scared. At that instant, firm hands grabbed Nina's arms and in one swift movement she was lifted onto the poolside, where she sat coughing and spluttering. Turning around to see her rescuer, she was baffled to find herself alone on the side of the pool. Everyone else was standing at the far end! Telling no one for fear of being laughed at, it was only in adulthood she realised that her guardian angel had been at hand that afternoon.

August 2

Angels are full of warmth and joy, and they always say the same thing – don't be afraid.

Sophy Burnham

Guiding Light Insight

Thoughts are bubbles of consciousness, like small capsules floating in space complete in themselves. Thoughts become truths and self-fulfilling prophecies.

Daily Affirmation

Today, my ideas are perfect and I successfully act upon them.

August 3

Divine Key

Take responsibility for your past, release what you
don't want, and program your thoughts with what
you do want.

Blessing

*May the Angel of Calm bring me balance and
mindfulness.*

August 4

It was an incredibly hot day and giving a reiki treatment was the last thing that Karen felt like doing. Her treatment room was quite small and stuffy, even with a cold air fan blowing. However, the lady on the telephone had sounded desperate and Karen had not had the heart to refuse her. Giving her client a glass of water before they started, Karen chatted a little with her. Opening up unexpectedly, the lady told Karen that her marriage had recently broken up and that she was struggling to cope alone. A good friend had recommended reiki as a source of calming treatment.

Settling the lady on her treatment table, Karen began to feel guilty for having had such negative thoughts earlier in the day. 'Sorry, angels,' she said silently. 'Please be with me as I try to help this distressed lady.' Suddenly an intense bright light filled the little room, even though Karen had closed the blinds against the sun. From this light, there radiated feelings of pure love and Karen found tears streaming down her face. Her client, lying with her eyes closed, saw nothing but later told Karen that it was the most incredible experience of her life – that she had felt surrounded by love.

August 5

There is a light that shines beyond all things on Earth. Beyond us all, beyond the heavens, beyond the very highest heavens.

CHANDOGYA UPANISHAD

Guiding Light Insight

The awakening of the spirit is a process that involves releasing ourselves from the material, physical realm and allowing ourselves to float upward to find the space and perspective we need. Thus, we bring spirit down to earth and raise earth into heaven.

Daily Affirmation

Today, I have self-belief in my life.

August 6

Divine Key

Know that you are one with all. Trust yourself to access the guidance, power, and wisdom of the higher realms.

Blessing

May the Angel of Miracles create unlimited possibilities in my life.

August 7

We would like to share with you the following thoughts of Revd John Harley:

> I have often been blessed over the years by experiences, sometimes seemingly mundane. A word from a stranger, which on reflection was a message I needed to hear. There were times when I have gained a flicker of strength from some presence. I have memories of catching glimpses of insight or grace or hope, or light, as if out of nowhere, or the magical and transforming awareness of a sign that seems to heal or save me. Some experiences seem crisp and real, yet are difficult to explain and perhaps unnecessary to try and analyse.
>
> Often it is a challenge to find the words and the language to explain such things. My theory is that some people, for a myriad of reasons, see some of these experiences as angels at work in their lives.

August 8

Last night I noticed that the pavement shone like a vast conurbation of diamonds in the evening darkness. In those precious moments, the frost had become more than a physical phenomenon, the glittery effect somehow lit me up inside, moved me and filled me with wonder.

JOHN HARLEY

Guiding Light Insight

The pain, upset or terror we may face is simply a reflection of the degree to which we are dependent and attached.

Daily Affirmation

Today, I accept peace and wholeness. I honour and respect myself.

August 9

Divine Key

No one is the same as anyone else, yet we all share a
common humanity.

Blessing

*May the Angel of Art bring unlimited beauty into
my life.*

August 10

Robert had booked a holiday in France as a surprise for his wife Liza, to celebrate their silver wedding anniversary. They enjoyed a wonderful anniversary party with family and close friends, and only that night did Robert tell his wife where they were going.

The holiday cottage proved to be delightful, situated in a beautiful spot on the coast. At the end of the first week, the couple decided to explore the surrounding countryside. As they sat in the hire car, they chatted about the party and Liza said that her only regret about it concerned her cousin Susan, who had been her bridesmaid. It would have been special to have had her there that night, Liza explained. However, Susan had gone to live in Canada years ago and the women had simply lost touch.

The car climbed higher into the mountains. At last reaching the top of a particularly high peak, they found a remote village with one tiny café. Entering the café, they noticed just one other couple inside enjoying lunch. For a moment, the two couples looked at each other silently. Then there was a loud gasp: it was Liza's cousin Susan and her husband!

August 11

Hold the fleet angel fast until he bless thee.

Nathaniel Cotton

Guiding Light Insight

A challenge is an obstacle on our way to somewhere.
It is a test that we must pass before we've earned the
right to get there.

Daily Affirmation

Today, serenity is the way of my life.

August 12

Divine Key

In order to please others, do you adopt roles that enable others to control you, to keep you imprisoned, or deny your rights? If you do, what is your reward or the pay-off you receive for being stuck in limitation?

Blessing

May the Angel of Prayer bring me peace.

August 13

Reaching twenty-one is a milestone in anyone's life and Megan looked forward to her celebrations. She was planning to have a party but on her actual birthday her immediate family were going to have a quiet meal together in a country pub. It was a bright, sunny Sunday when the family set off.

After a wonderful lunch, the family was ushered into a lounge for coffee and Megan opened some of the gifts she had been given that day. One was a statue of an angel with white wings outstretched. It made Megan exclaim with pleasure. 'She is so keen on angels,' Megan's mum later explained, 'that it was a perfect gift.' At this point Megan's father took a few photos of the family before turning to Megan and saying, 'One of you by yourself now, love.'

The following morning, Megan took the film to be developed in her lunch break. Collecting them an hour later, she gasped as she looked through them. For there was the photograph that her father had taken of her alone, yet standing behind her was a perfect angel.

August 14

From friendship, Angels gather half their joy.

EDWARD YOUNG

Guiding Light Insight

Mastery requires us to acquire a high tolerance for
discomfort, for risk-taking and for venturing into the
unknown. The line of least resistance can be
valuable at times, but it can also be limiting.

Daily Affirmation

*Today, I take risks and expand beyond my
present comfort zone.*

August 15

Divine Key

How you perceive yourself and what you hold to be
the purpose and meaning of life will determine how
you deal with your challenges and how you label
your experiences.

Blessing

May the Angel of Change give me courage to let
go and accept the new.

August 16

It was a very hot summer's day. Nine-year-old Marina and her aunts sat in the shade of a vine at her grandmother's house on the beautiful Portuguese island of Madeira. The house and garden were surrounded by a large stone wall and the entrance was protected by a very heavy wooden oak door. It offered privacy but also obscured the view of the narrow street outside.

It was time for Marina to go home and walk the short distance to her own house nearby. Walking up the stone steps that led to the garden door, she waved goodbye to her aunts. At that moment Marina heard a terrible noise. She was aware of strong arms holding her as she felt herself pulled swiftly away from the door. With a crashing sound the stone walls fell as a huge lorry came thundering through, knocking flat the heavy oak door. It fell only inches in front of Marina and on the exact spot she had been standing seconds before! Dust, noise, and screams of terror filled the air, but all Marina could hear was a sweet musical voice in her ear say, 'It's all right, you are safe.' She has no doubt that this was her guardian angel.

August 17

God committed the care of men and all things under heaven to Angels.

JUSTIN MARTYR

Guiding Light Insight

Miracles start to occur when we begin to follow where our heart leads. If we are true to ourselves and move in the direction of our bliss, we will manifest what we love.

Daily Affirmation

Today I acknowledge my worth and I treat myself with respect.

August 18

Divine Key

Your attitude is everything, for without excitement
and enthusiasm nothing really happens.

Blessing

*May the Angel of Nature bring me promise and
resurrection.*

August 19

This is our second story about Marina, whom we met on 16 August. It illustrates how she was protected throughout her childhood. Marina says she heard the same voice in this incident too, convincing her that it belongs to her own personal angel.

Playing happily one day near to her home, Marina accidentally fell into a deep lake. She had not yet learned to swim and was totally petrified with fear. Then the mysterious voice spoke again in her ear, and once more she had the feeling of being supported. The voice told her not to be afraid as she would be taken care of. Floating on the water for some time, Marina finally alerted a man who was working in the nearby fields. He pulled her to safety.

Marina grew up to become a journalist and radio presenter for RTP Madeira, but she has had a strong sense of her angel being close to her every single day since those childhood incidents.

August 20

She felt again that small shiver that occurred to her when events hinted at destiny being played out, of unseen forces intervening.

DOROTHY GILMAN

Guiding Light Insight

Everything is moving, changing, and flowing each and every moment. When we begin to view our lives as living art, one moment flows into the next.

Daily Affirmation

Today, I proclaim myself to be whole, complete and perfect.

August 21

Divine Key

Self-esteem, self-love and self-worth are essential,
for love is what we are. We are the frequency of love,
and the more we allow ourselves to love ourselves
and to receive love, the more love we will have to
direct outwards.

Blessing

May the Angel of Innocence bring me complete

synchronicity.

August 22

This little story happened one day when Glennyce welcomed a friend round for coffee. In the course of their conversation Glennyce and Diane talked about symbolism, especially in the world of nature. They concluded that birds such as the robin seem to be particularly symbolic.

Leaving Glennyce, Diane went to the chapel garden where she had scattered her husband's ashes some months before. She had a few quiet moments in the garden and returned to her car. Aware of a rustling in a nearby bush, she looked hopefully for a robin; it was however a little brown thrush. Preparing to drive away, Diane looked through the car window and there, sitting on the pavement staring directly at her, was a beautiful robin with piercing eyes! Catching her breath in wonder, she stared at this lovely bird, but it did not move. At last, starting the car slowly in order to turn around in the narrow street, she drove gently to the main road. Glancing up, she saw the robin was now sitting on the chapel wall, watching her drive away. As with all these symbolic events, it is definitely in the timing!

August 23

My father explained to me, 'All things in this world,' he said, 'have souls or spirits. The sky has a spirit, the clouds have spirits, the sun and moon have spirits, so have animals, trees, grass, water, stars, everything.'

DANTE ALIGGHIER

Guiding Light Insight

When our professional or personal lives become too demanding, we would do well to be still. In this way, we may receive insights from our higher selves which will show us how to proceed for our greater good.

Daily Affirmation

Today, I honour the temple of my body by treating it with tender, loving care.

August 24

Divine Key

Starting today, stand up for your decisions and be clear about your purpose and intention.

Blessing

May the Angel of Order choose perfect situations for me.

August 25

Our next story about the symbolism of birds comes not from an English garden but from Smolensk in Russia. It was the funeral of Olga's close friend Lyononchka, and Olga had followed the coffin as mourners strewed flowers in its path. It is customary in this part of the world to bring a funeral wreath of flowers to the grave nine days after the burial. Completing this sad task, Olga and friends now sat on a bench near their friend's home, talking about him and their shared memories.

Literally out of the blue, a flock of cranes flew up from the waters of the Dnieper river. This was odd because in August all the other migratory birds had long gone. These birds then appeared to hover, almost stationary, above Lyononchka's house. The birds circled so low, they were almost touching the roof of the house and remained above it for what seemed like a long time before forming the familiar triangle formation and flying away over the river. Olga says she will never forget that August day as long as she lives, firmly believing the flight of the cranes was a sign from her friend.

August 26

Birds have since ancient times represented the soul and the ability to deliver messages from the departed loved one.

ANONYMOUS

Guiding Light Insight

Our thoughts of lack manifest as limitations, whereas our thoughts of abundance manifest as success.

Daily Affirmation

Today, I listen with an open heart.

August 27

Divine Key

Giving and receiving are a part of the same process of universal circulation. The receiver must give, and the giver must receive in order to stay healthy.

Blessing

May the Angel of Service bring me balance.

August 28

As we have seen, symbolism is a powerful force in life. It can take many forms and in Myrna's story it comes in the form of a compelling dream. Myrna's father had sadly died on her birthday, which did not entirely come as a shock as Myrna had already heard a mysterious voice telling her this would be the case.

A few months later she experienced a very lucid dream. In it, a large 'being' (which Myrna thought might be a guardian angel) sheltered two men under his wings, one of whom was Myrna's father. Myrna's father appeared to be completely restored to health and his face glowed a robust brown, a blend of all human skin colours.

In her dream Myrna was wrapped in a huge bath towel that had been given to her as a special gift for her twenty-first birthday. It felt like an honour when the angel kissed the hem of her towel. She felt it was a symbol of cleansing and purification in her life. It was not until Myrna began to tell this story to Glennyce that she realised there was a more profound symbolism to it all. Her father had become a Christian only months before he died, so could the central figure in the triptych have been Jesus, representing healing? It is a dream Myrna will never forget.

August 29

Surely no one can still believe that dreams are no more than illusions, tricks played by the mind without significance or purpose? We would simply not dream, if dreams served no useful end.

PIERRE DACO

Guiding Light Insight

As human beings with emotions, we are susceptible to getting hurt. But that same susceptibility is what also allows us to experience life.

Daily Affirmation

Today, I love with an open heart.

August 30

Divine Key

Dreams are messages from our souls. If we listen to
their messages and consider their symbols, we may
learn much about ourselves.

Blessing

May the Angel of Dreams guide me.

August 31

The interview had gone very well and Donna was convinced she had secured the job. However, she was extremely nervous about moving to London from her home in Liverpool. She did not know a soul in London and the thought of trying to find accommodation filled her with dread. But she felt that at the age of twenty-four it was time for her to break away from the comfort of family and friends, and to strike out on her own.

Boarding the train back home to Liverpool, Donna had very mixed feelings. A smiling lady occupied the seat opposite and soon they struck up a conversation. Donna found herself telling this complete stranger all her troubles. The lady listened intently until Donna had finished. She then told Donna she was on her way to visit her daughter who was at university in Liverpool. She recalled how nervous her daughter had been moving from home for the first time. Delving into her handbag, she then handed Donna a card with her details on it and said, 'I have a large house in London with several spare rooms, if you would like to stay with me you are more than welcome!'

Two years later, Donna is still happily living with her lovely friend, and firmly believes the angels placed her on the train that day.

September 1

To angels, home is not only where the heart is but all hearts.

KAREN GOLDMAN

Guiding Light Insight

We have the ability to know great truths and to follow our intuition. It is what we do with this information that makes life interesting.

Daily Affirmation

Today, I am in perfect grace and ease in every situation.

September 2

Divine Key

Once you have removed your energy and your attention from a problem, and allowed a flow of new energy to it, the solution will appear.

Blessing

May the Angel of Joy create a path of positive energy and success for me and those I love.

September 3

Kath's family were visiting Cyprus for a wedding on 1 September 2005. A few days prior to the wedding, strange events began to happen to the visitors. Kath explained how her brother was woken from sleep by a tap on his shoulder. When he opened his eyes, he just had time to prevent the heavy wooden head-board from his bed falling on top of him and his partner.

The following night Kath retired early, knowing the wedding day would be long and tiring, albeit happy. Waking in the early hours, she went to pour herself a glass of water. As she glanced across the room, she saw a hazy figure wearing a white shirt and black bow tie. This was what the men would wear to the wedding, so Kath assumed that her partner, Mark, must have hung his clothes outside the wardrobe. However, climbing back into bed she looked closely at the figure again. It was clearly not Mark's clothing and so she whispered, 'Is that you, Dad?' All of the family missed Kath's father, who had died four years earlier. However, the morning of the big day revealed that the wardrobe doors were shut, with Mark's clothing locked away behind them!

After the long wedding celebrations, the family all went back to their apartments, to find the balcony doors of all family rooms had been flung open wide. The rooms were several floors above ground level, had been left firmly locked, and no one had been inside those rooms all day. Everyone concluded that these were signs that Kath's father had indeed attended his granddaughter's wedding.

September 4

Look at the stars! look look up at the skies!
O at all the fire-folk sitting in the air!
The bright boroughs, the citadels there!

GERARD MANLEY HOPKINS

Guiding Light Insight

Every person has a god-like energy and divine qualities.

Daily Affirmation

Today, there is nothing for me to guard against.

September 5

Divine Key

Our lives are precious and we are made of the same
substance as the stars.

Blessing

May the Angel of Mystic Energy fill me with
wellbeing and health.

September 6

We have been fortunate enough to acquire many wonderful stories about rainbows, some of which you will have read earlier in this book.

Marie's rainbow story is unique and uplifting. It had been a dreadful time in her life. A long relationship had come to an end and she had been forced to find somewhere new to live. Now Marie was feeling lower than she could ever recall having felt before. The little house that she had moved into was, in her own words, 'quite grim'. It was a struggle to come to terms with all the sad changes in her life.

One morning, as Marie climbed the little stairs to her bedroom, her sense of despair was overwhelming. However, as she entered the room, she gasped in astonishment for the whole room was filled with rainbows! Confused as well as delighted, Marie opened the curtains to find that the day outside was unrelentingly grey. The rainbows were the most wonderful message that all would be well after her own personal storm. Indeed, they marked a turning point and life has continued to improve for Marie. Each day she asks the angels for help and, she says, they always answer.

September 7

Rainbows were believed to be a bridge over which departed souls travelled to heaven. A divine symbol linking earth to heaven.

I.S. JONES

Guiding Light Insight

Everything in life is a reflection of what is taking place at the level of pure spirit.

Daily Affirmation

Today, I allow all my ideas, thoughts and feelings to take form in matter.

September 8

Divine Key

There is hope that you can manifest your true heart's desire if you are willing to seek out and apply the spiritual principles that will help to make your dreams come true.

Blessing

May the Angel of Wishes fulfil my cherished dreams.

September 9

Grandparents and grandchildren often share a very special bond. This was certainly true for Anthony and his grandfather. A music teacher, Anthony's grandfather had taught him to play the piano and violin, and had instilled in him the love of music from an early age. Anthony's grandfather's funeral had naturally included lots of music and Anthony had played a violin piece by Vivaldi that they both loved.

Just a few weeks after the funeral, Anthony celebrated his twenty-first birthday. He was deeply sad his grandfather could not have been there. Arriving home in the early hours of the morning after an excellent party, Anthony was getting ready for bed, when suddenly his bedroom was filled with music. It was their favourite Vivaldi piece. There seemed to be no logical source for it: Anthony had not switched on his CD player or the radio. The music sounded ethereal. No one else in the house heard anything and Anthony concluded that this was his grandfather's way of telling him he was with him on his special birthday.

September 10

The soul should always stand ajar,
Ready to welcome the ecstatic experience.

EMILY DICKINSON

Guiding Light Insight

When we allow our hearts to open to others, we
create something precious and eternal.

Daily Affirmation

Today, I fill my life with joy and laughter.

September 11

Divine Key

The world around us is an outward manifestation of our inner worlds of mental concepts, beliefs and assumptions. What we choose to believe will appear in our outer world much as a movie is projected onto a big screen.

Blessing

May the Angel of Effective Guidance always bring me feelings of love, joy and passion.

September 12

As we have seen, celestial phenomena such as rainbows are often important heavenly signs. Clouds also feature as symbols of hope in many angel stories.

Facing an important decision, Paula was having difficulty sleeping and rose very early in the morning to go for a walk. She was visiting the stunningly beautiful island of Tenerife, and trying to decide if she and her husband should live there permanently. But such a long-distance move from England entailed many different considerations and now all those details swirled around in her head.

The morning was glorious as she left the apartment. There was not a soul in sight, only deep blue skies and the sound of the waves. Walking along, deep in thought, Paula was oblivious to the surrounding beauty and stared at the ground as she walked. Halting suddenly, she looked up into the sky and gasped, for the entire sky – which had been totally clear moments before – was now filled with tiny, perfect, feather-shaped clouds! She knew instantly that this was a sign that she was meant to live in that wonderful place.

September 13

My soul is awakened, my spirit is soaring
And carried aloft on the wings of the breeze.

ANNE BRONTË

Guiding Light Insight

If we only speak nurturing and empowering words to
others, we will only create loving relationships.

Daily Affirmation

Today, I open my heart and let my spirit speak to
me.

September 14

Divine Key

The presence of love is a healing power. The effects
of this healing are quite profound, and can be experienced in every aspect of our lives.

Blessing

*May the Angel of Eternal Consciousness make a
difference in my outer world.*

September 15

During pregnancy there are several worries that are common to all mothers-to-be, with the health of the baby being a primary concern for many. When Kath was pregnant she had an overwhelming feeling that her baby would be born with spina bifida. This unshakeable belief stayed with her right up to the moment of her baby's birth. Matthew was indeed born with the condition, but he was a beautiful child and much loved by the whole family. When Matthew was only four weeks old he had to undergo surgery. Tragically, he did not survive the operation and the resulting heartbreak was dreadful for Kath and her family. But Kath was always grateful to have had him for even such a short time and after his death she felt that he was close to her.

Some years later Kath attended a spiritual festival. During a workshop she was led into a visualisation. It was a powerful and lucid experience, and suddenly she saw Matthew, now grown into a young man in heaven. He told Kath that her destiny was to help people, that she must trust and love him and to be aware that he was with her always. He added that she must trust her instincts and follow her path. The image was so overwhelming that later Kath needed counselling by the workshop leader. However, her life was never to be the same again. She has since qualified in many types of therapy and helps hundreds of people. Matthew is her guide and indicates his closeness and support constantly.

September 16

Suffer the little children to come unto me ...
For of such is the Kingdom of Heaven.

MATTHEW 19:14

Guiding Light Insight

To increase our faith, we should pay attention to our
little successes at first. And when we see the results,
we should celebrate them.

Daily Affirmation

Today, I set my intentions, expand my faith and
accept greater results.

September 17

Divine Key

To move yourself out of doubt and into faith, you
must start right where you are. Begin with what you
know and go from there.

Blessing

May the Angel of Desired Faith overcome
my doubts and fears.

September 18

Here is an intriguing excerpt from *Heaven and Hell*, a book by the mystic and theologian Emanuel Swedenborg:

Many may suppose that in heaven little children remain little children, and continue as such among the angels. Those who do not know what an angel is may have had this opinion confirmed by paintings and images in churches, in which angels are represented as children. But it is wholly otherwise. Intelligence and wisdom are what constitute an angel, and as long as children do not possess these they are not angels, although they are with the angels; but as soon as they become intelligent and wise they become angels; and what is wonderful, they do not then appear as children, but as adults, for they are no longer of an infantile genius, but of a more mature angelic genius. Intelligence and wisdom produce this effect. The reason why children appear more mature, thus as youths or young men, as they are perfected in intelligence and wisdom, is that intelligence and wisdom are essential spiritual nourishment; and thus the things that nourish their minds also nourish their bodies, and this from correspondence; for the form of the body is simply the external form of the interiors. But it should be understood that in heaven children advance in age only to early manhood and remain in this to eternity.

September 19

To change one's life; start immediately. Do it flamboyantly. No exceptions.

WILLIAM JAMES

Guiding Light Insight

If we accept ourselves and others exactly the way we are, we leave open the possibility for greater expression, and free ourselves from sitting in judgement.

Daily Affirmation

Today, I accept unconditional love. I love myself and trust myself.

September 20

Divine Key

Use the energy of desire to attract what makes life meaningful and wonderful for you. Once you have accepted miracles in this way, you can help to transform others.

Blessing

May the Angel of Acceptance transform my life into something wonderful.

September 21

Travelling alone over long distances can be very stressful. About to fly for the first time, Valerie was excited and petrified in equal measure! After a great deal of persuasion, she had agreed to visit her son and his family in Australia. The first challenge came when Valerie flew from London to Amsterdam, where she had to change planes for the long haul flight. As she alighted in Amsterdam, she was literally shaking. An elderly gentleman approached her and asked if she was feeling unwell. Valerie explained her circumstances and the old gentleman told her to follow him. With his white hair and twinkling blue eyes, the old gentleman filled her with calm and courage. Guiding her through the airport procedure, he took Valerie to the departure lounge for her connecting flight. When her flight was called Valerie took the boarding pass from her handbag, then turned to shake hands with the old man, who had been sitting beside her. But he had completely vanished.

When she asked a lady sitting a little further down the row if she had seen where the man had gone, the woman looked puzzled and said that the seats had all been empty apart from that occupied by Valerie!

September 22

Feel the fear and do it anyway.

SUSAN JEFFERS

Guiding Light Insight
By setting our intention, we can shape destiny.

Daily Affirmation
Today, I let gratitude embrace my life.

September 23

Divine Key
When you know that you can have what you want,
it becomes easy to support others in having what
they want.

Blessing

*May the Angel of Life bring me Infinite
Intelligence.*

September 24

After just one month in her new role Carole began to think that she had found her perfect job. Her colleagues were warm and friendly; the salary represented a huge increase; in short, she was extremely happy. However, the job was very demanding and there was a lot of new information for Carole to remember. She decided the best way to cope would be to buy a large notebook and jot down every detail. This proved to be an extremely valuable practice.

One morning Carole called in at her local newsagent's and bought several items, which she placed in her bag. Sometime later in the office, she discovered her large notebook was missing. It had definitely been in her bag when she left home. She concluded in panic that she must have lost it in the newsagent's. However, it had not been seen in the shop, and she searched her home thoroughly without success before dissolving into tears.

That night she prayed as never before, asking God to send an angel to help. Arriving in the office the following morning, she could scarcely believe her eyes, for there in the middle of her desk was the precious notebook! All staff assured her they had not placed it there, as no one had even been aware that she had lost it. Carole silently thanked God and his angels for their timely intervention.

September 25

Angels exist through the eyes of faith, and faith is perception. Only if you can perceive it can you experience it.

JOHN WESTERHOFF

Guiding Light Insight

If we do something every day that is related to our greater goals in life, our intention, commitment and actions will quickly produce the results we are looking for.

Daily Affirmation

Today, I step confidently out of my comfort zone.

September 26

Divine Key

Your preconceived expectations and labels simply limit you and keep you from what could be yours.

Blessing

May the Angel of Sunshine bring me value and purpose.

September 27

When writing one of our books we often come across several stories that are very similar in content. Recently we have received numerous accounts of divine intervention for little children and babies in danger, such as the tale that follows here.

Peeping in at Thomas as she went to bed, Helen smiled at her beautiful sleeping child. Climbing into bed after a busy day, she fell into deep sleep. Some time later Helen was awakened by a voice softly calling her name. Sleepily she opened her eyes to find an empty room.

Her husband was away on business and Helen was alone in the house except for her baby. Immediately she fell back onto her pillow and closed her eyes, knowing she would fall asleep instantly. However, the voice called her name loudly this time and she sat up with a start. The room was still empty but this time she left her bed and went to Thomas's room. She was horrified to find that the little boy had slipped beneath his cot blankets and was struggling to breathe! Untangling him, she hugged him tightly and realised how close to tragedy they had been. Helen thanked her angel because there simply could have been no other explanation for that wonderful wake-up call.

September 28

Once a dream did weave a shade,
O'er my angel-guarded bed.

WILLIAM BLAKE

Guiding Light Insight

We can act in the confidence that everything will
work out for our highest good and for the highest
good of all.

Daily Affirmation

Today, I push through all my obstacles.

September 29

Divine Key

Nothing dies in the Universe: energy simply changes form.

Blessing

May the Angel of Energy give me a strategic plan.

September 30

The autumn equinox arrives and nature changes its colours, providing us with beauty and a time for reflection.

Exercise for the Autumn Equinox

As the seasons turn we automatically compare them with our lives. We all grow older but each stage in life brings its own beauty and rewards, as does each season in nature.

Reflect upon where you are in your life. Are there any ambitions that you used to cherish, but which no longer seem so important to you now? What are the priorities in your life today? What fruits from the past can you reap today? Is there anything that you could do without and that you are ready to shed, as the trees shed their autumn leaves? Enjoy the wonders of the season and consider how it relates to your own life.

October 1

Angels from the Lord lead and protect us every
moment and every moment of every moment.

 EMANUEL SWEDENBORG

Guiding Light Insight

Our lives have their seasons and we too are a part of
the natural world.

Daily Affirmation

Today, I create beauty, harmony and perfection in
all areas in my life.

October 2

Meditation for the Autumn

Sit in a warm, comfortable place in your house and relax. Picture yourself in a wood where the trees are just beginning to change their colour. The early morning sky is deep blue and the sun shines down through the leaves. Walk slowly down the woodland path until you reach a clearing. In front of you is a small waterfall that makes a beautiful gentle sound as the water reaches the rocks below. As you gaze, a figure in a long blue gown emerges and beckons you to go forward. She holds out a gift for you in her hand. Approach her and gratefully take the gift from her. Study it closely as you hold it in your hand. This is exactly what you wish for this morning to help you through the day. Thank your angel and return down the beautiful woodland path, secure in the knowledge that you are loved.

October 3

The greatest gift that you can give yourself
Is a little bit of your own attention.

Anthony J. Angelo

Guiding Light Insight
We are the embodiment of Universal Love.

Daily Affirmation
Today, I let go of my negative habits and the
destructive patterns in my life.

October 4

Divine Key

Every time you contribute money, enjoy giving it in the knowledge that as you give, so shall you receive.

Blessing

May the Angel of Plenty bring prosperity and bounty into my life.

October 5

Portugal can be fiercely hot in the summer, as Lisa and her family discovered. One day on holiday, she found the heat almost too much. The family struggled back to the hotel for a rest. Exhausted, they arrived back and gratefully sank onto the sofas. Lisa's little boy was just three years old and toddled into his adjoining room. Suddenly Lisa had a picture in her head of her child leaning out of the window. Knowing there was a drop of four stories from the window onto concrete, it was an uncomfortable vision. However, she immediately dismissed the image from her mind because she knew for certain she had locked all windows and doors on leaving that morning. The vision persisted, however, and she jumped up and ran to the other room.

There was her vision unfolding before her eyes: her little boy was indeed leaning out of the window, perilously close to falling. She grabbed hold of him just in time to prevent a tragedy. It appeared that the maid had opened the window in their absence. To this day, Lisa thanks her angels for the insistent vision.

October 6

Angel protection is open to everyone.

CURTIS SLIWA

Guiding Light Insight

We must all start where we are currently, in order to approach our ultimate goals.

Daily Affirmation

Today, I live in gratitude and serenity.

October 7

Divine Key

**You must get in touch with your heart to discover
what you really want from life.**

Blessing

*May the Angel of Reason help me to let go of any
blame, excuses and justifications in my life.*

October 8

The entire Walker family decided to have their annual holiday together. They rented a huge villa in the Tuscan countryside and everyone looked forward to the occasion immensely. The youngest member of the clan was little Laura, who was five years old and full of mischief. She was thrilled at the prospect of having seven cousins to play with for a whole three weeks.

The holiday was going very well. One hot day they discovered a lovely village nearby where they could eat lunch outdoors. Laura looked around and to her delight saw several horses in the field opposite. In an instant, she leaped from her chair and ran towards them. It was a very quiet village but the café was on the main street. At that very moment a fast car came hurtling around the bend. Everyone dashed towards Laura and they were extremely relieved to see she had jumped backwards from the road in the nick of time.

Hugs and scolding followed. Her mother told her sternly that she was a very lucky little girl. Through her tears, Laura said, 'I know. Who pulled me back?' Her mother asked what she meant and Laura said a firm hand had grabbed her shoulder and pulled her out of the car's way. But everyone had seen that Laura was by herself when she avoided the car. They all fell silent. Her mother knew the source of such help.

October 9

The wind was in their wings.

ZECHARIAH 5:9

Guiding Light Insight

The more energy that we allow to flow through us,
the more we will experience and participate in life.

Daily Affirmation

Today, I set forth my ideas and goals.

October 10

Divine Key

Look at your life to see what you have completed
and what remains uncompleted.

Blessing

*May the Angel of Completion heal and give me
oneness with the Universe.*

October 11

Lisa is the first to admit that her sense of direction is less than perfect. That, added to that fact that she was in a strange city thousands of miles from home, meant that it was almost inevitable she would get lost. Brisbane was a new and exciting experience, but when Lisa realised that it was time to rejoin her husband at their agreed meeting place she also discovered that she had no idea how to get there. The situation deteriorated when she suddenly found herself in a completely deserted street with no means of contacting her husband.

Panic was setting in and Lisa did the only thing she could think of: she asked for help from above. From nowhere a man appeared just ahead of her, walking briskly down the street. As it had seemed like such a marvellous coincidence to see him appear at the precise moment that she had asked for help, Lisa ran to follow him. Sure enough, her confidence was rewarded when he led her straight to where her husband was waiting for her. Angels truly come in all guises.

October 12

*The angels are ordered to answer the prayers of
the believers.*

IMAM SALIK

Guiding Light Insight

**What we give our attention to increases, fed by the
Universal law of attraction.**

Daily Affirmation

*Today, my future is full of incredible
opportunities.*

October 13

Divine Key
You have all the wisdom and choices you need to
take control of any situation.

Blessing
*May the Angel of Spiritual Secrets give me
unlimited inspiration.*

October 14

Our next story is most definitely of the 'spiritual coincidence' category. Whenever these things happen we are left marvelling at the divine timing. Catherine says that one Thursday in October, a few years ago, her mother died in the local nursing home. They were informed that the time of her death was 12.50 a.m. Feeling terribly sad, the family gathered in Catherine's kitchen, feeling in need of a strong drink! At this point Catherine's sister decided to ring their Aunt Margaret. As the only surviving contemporary of their mother, Margaret would need to know about the death. When Catherine's sister came back into the room she looked shocked. It transpired that Aunt Margaret had also died that morning at 12.30 a.m.

The following day an old friend was contacted, only for the women to discover that she too had died on that October Thursday. Catherine says that these three ladies may not have been the best of friends at the time of death but she likes to think of them reunited, arm in arm skipping into heaven!

October 15

Forgiveness is the great release from time, it is the key to learning that the past is over.

A COURSE IN MIRACLES

Guiding Light Insight

The veil between spirit and matter is very thin. As spiritual beings we must live for today, and have no regrets in this life. Life is truly in this moment, and in this moment we must celebrate ourselves and acknowledge others.

Daily Affirmation

Today, I claim perfect health, perfect relationships, perfect, ever-flowing abundance in my life.

October 16

Divine Key

Courage is a way of living in the world, and it can be
brought to bear on any situation.

Blessing

May the Angel of Harmony
free me from worry.

October 17

Visiting Japan with her elderly mother was the highlight of Avril's life. They stayed with Avril's brother, who was working in the country. It was a magical experience: the beauty of the countryside, especially the multi-coloured chrysanthemums flowering everywhere, took their breath away. 'No wonder they are the national flower of Japan,' her brother said.

Only weeks after this wonderful visit, Avril's mother died. When her brother arrived for the funeral they both agreed that it had been such a blessing to have shared a holiday with her so recently. The morning after the funeral, Avril's brother went for a little walk in the garden. On returning to the house he said, 'How lovely to see you have beautiful chrysanthemums in the garden – a reminder of Mum and your visit to Japan.' Astonished at this remark, Avril rushed outside. There were indeed wonderful chrysanthemum flowers blooming in the garden.

'They certainly were not there yesterday,' she said, 'I have never grown those flowers in the garden!'

'Well,' replied her brother, 'it must have been Mum's first act as an angel.'

October 18

The flower is the holiest and most divine of all the gifts bestowed on us.

JOHN RUSKIN

Guiding Light Insight

As we travel on our journey we will find other like-minded people to support and uplift us, but ultimately each one of us is responsible for our own future.

Daily Affirmation

Today, I choose to accept myself.

October 19

Divine Key

**You are attuned to the frequency of love, in harmony
with the Universe. Give love and receive love.**

Blessing

*May the Angel of Diligence give me the insight to
accomplish all that I desire.*

October 20

Researching the family tree is a very popular pastime today. Such research reveals that the population is shifting. No longer do extended families live close together, but on leaving university sons and daughters often find jobs a long way from their childhood homes.

Rosemary had the sudden urge to discover more details about her long lost relatives. The trail of her great-grandfather led her to Scotland and a small border town. As she had grown up on the south coast of England, this was her first visit to Scotland. However, with regard to finding out more about the family, it was proving to be very disappointing. All areas of enquiry proved fruitless and after several days Rosemary gave up and packed her car for the drive home.

Deciding to take a look at the sea before heading south, Rosemary found herself by a beautiful stretch of coast. She walked up to a cliff top where she sat on a bench to drink in the view. 'Well, great-grandfather,' she said aloud, 'I did try! Wherever you are, God bless.' Rising from the bench, she noticed a dedication plaque on the back of it. It read: 'In memory of Gregory Sinclaire', and there were his dates and some further details. Rosemary caught her breath – the bench was dedicated to her great-grandfather!

October 21

*No accident or chance is possible within the
Universe as God created it, outside of which is
nothing.*

A COURSE IN MIRACLES

Guiding Light Insight

An open attitude to life offers us a full range of
experiences, whereas a closed one offers us
very little.

Daily Affirmation

Today, I am making profound changes in my life.

October 22

Divine Key

Spiritual mastery requires that we have a high tolerance for being uncomfortable, and for risk-taking and for venturing into the unknown.

Blessing

May the Angel of Alliance give me the

opportunity to own more of myself.

October 23

Saying goodbye to those we love is never easy and Pat was feeling very sad. Her father had been in a retirement home for four years and although this had been a very happy time for him, clearly the end was now approaching. He was very ill indeed the afternoon that Pat went to visit him. As she approached his bed, he turned to her and said, 'Did you see him?'

Puzzled, Pat asked, 'Who?

'The man in the dark suit,' he replied. 'He just came into the room and asked me if I was ready to go. I told him, "No, not at the moment." He must have left as you arrived, through the open door.'

The following day, Pat's father died and she took great comfort in the thought that the mysterious man may have been an old friend coming to meet him.

October 24

The journey to God is merely a reawakening of the knowledge of where you are always, and what you are forever. It is a journey without distance, to a goal that has never changed.

A Course in Miracles

Guiding Light Insight

We must understand that there is no death and that our bodies only change their energetic form. Our last breath here on earth is the first breath on another journey.

Daily Affirmation

Today, I create new patterns of being, relating and living.

October 25

Divine Key

How you think about yourself is more important
than how others think about you. Our own thoughts
create situations and events that take place in our
lives and no one else's belief affects you but your
own.

Blessing

May the Angel of Sharing fill my heart

with love.

October 26

At just twelve months old, Christopher was full of fun and into everything. His mother Sandra only really relaxed once he was safely tucked up in bed each night. One sunny afternoon, Sandra took her baby to an open area of grass to enjoy the fresh air. After a little time, she delved into her handbag to retrieve a drink for the little boy, momentarily taking her eyes off him. Looking up, she saw to her horror that Christopher was rolling out of control down a steep slope directly in the path of several girls on horseback. The girls rode along swiftly, chatting to each other and oblivious to the baby. As if this were not enough danger, Sandra was aware of a large, fierce-looking dog bounding towards her baby.

Scrambling down the slope as fast as she could, Sandra said out loud, 'God help me!' The dog reached the tumbling baby, seized him in his mouth by his clothing and pulled him out of harm's way. The horses galloped past and then the dog gently placed him back onto the grass! It all happened in an instant and Sandra scooped up her little boy, patted the dog and, with her heart racing, thanked God for his help.

October 27

In my defencelessness my safety lies.

A COURSE IN MIRACLES

Guiding Light Insight

If we could only love ourselves enough, we would know ourselves to be one with all that is now and forever.

Daily Affirmation

Today, I bring forth my natural creative power to inspire and heal my life.

October 28

Divine Key

The flow of the Divine moves through us and if we
believe in scarcity we close off the natural flow of
the Universe.

Blessing

*May the Angel of Principle bring me harmony
in all matters.*

October 29

Final exams were fast approaching for Duncan and the thought of them filled him with dread. His confidence was beginning to drain from him and he was convinced that his three years at university would soon be wasted when he failed miserably. Depression engulfed him like a black cloud and he found it difficult to talk to his family or friends about his problems. 'If only I could get help from somewhere,' he thought. Overcome with the enormity of it all, he decided to take a break to do what he enjoyed most, which was to go climbing. A day away from the problem might be beneficial, he reasoned.

Leaving the city revived his spirits somewhat and, longing to climb, he reached his chosen destination. He continued climbing until he reached the highest peaks. It was an area familiar to Duncan so even as darkness fell he experienced no fear. Instead, he felt engulfed with a strange feeling of peace and a warm glow. Looking up into the sky, he saw the clouds lift, revealing a wonderful panorama of stars. 'I am not religious,' he said later, 'but in that moment I knew God was with me and all would be well.' As a postscript, we are pleased to add that Duncan attained his degree.

October 30

No one in their right mind can see the stars and the eternal blackness everywhere and deny the spirituality of the experience, nor the existence of a supreme being. There were moments when I honestly felt that I could reach out my hand and touch the face of God.

EUGENE CERNAN, THE LAST MAN TO WALK ON THE MOON

Guiding Light Insight
Life is abundant in lessons and treasures that will come to us in exchange for our participation and the giving of our own gifts.

Daily Affirmation
Today, I am made vigorous and whole.

October 31

Divine Key

Every part of your body is in harmony with the living spirit.

Blessing

May the Angel of Boldness transform my dreams into reality.

November 1

Amy was having a wonderful time on holiday. Travelling around the Greek Islands with friends, she sent regular text messages home to her parents. Her mum, Janet, was a little concerned because she knew that Amy and her friends had hired scooters. However, the first week passed and all was well. The friends were apparently enjoying the freedom that riding a bike affords.

One night, Janet awoke with a start. Sitting up in bed, she could feel her heart racing and she had no idea why this should be. In the corner of her bedroom there appeared a light, which grew in intensity until it filled the whole room. As quickly as it had appeared, the light faded and Janet was left totally bemused but unafraid by the experience. Glancing at the clock and seeing that it was only 2.30 a.m., she promptly went back to sleep.

The next morning Janet received a phone call from her daughter, saying, 'Don't panic, Mum, but I'm in hospital. We had an accident last night, riding back to the hotel. I'm not seriously hurt but will have to spend a few days in here.'

'What time was this?' Janet asked. Working out the time difference, they calculated that the accident had taken place at 2.30 a.m. UK time!

November 2

The light in the dark,

The presence in our loneliness,

The strength in our weakness.

The guide in our lostness.

FROM THE BREASTPLATE OF SAINT PATRICK

Guiding Light Insight

The miracle of our lives is that we are here on earth. Our souls made a conscious choice to be here.

Daily Affirmation

Today, I create a sacred space for my family and myself.

November 3

Divine Key

When we embrace life's sacred possibilities, the
wiser we become.

Blessing

May the Angel of Nature bring honour
to our planet.

November 4

This is a great story about synchronicity that will make you smile!

Jan met Glennyce earlier this year when she attended a talk that Glennyce was giving. Jan lives in Lytham St Anne's, which is a pretty coastal town in Lancashire. While visiting friends some distance away, she found herself at a book sale in Padiham Unitarian Chapel. There were so many books for sale that Jan was mesmerised by them. Suddenly, she spotted a book with a lovely blue cover peeping out from a selection; she picked it up and found it was a copy of Glennyce's book *An Angel at My Shoulder*. This she bought.

Some days later Jan was back at work as a shop assistant in her home town, when a lady came into her shop and they started to talk about angels. The customer mentioned that she was going to hear someone speak about angels in nearby Blackpool. 'Her name is Glennyce, I think,' the woman said. Jan asked, 'Would that be Eckersley?'

'Yes,' the lady replied, and Jan said she would go with her. Later that day, Jan popped into the bookshop next door to her place of work, to look at the selection of angel books. On the shelf directly in front of these books, she found a large white feather. 'Do you put white feathers into your angel books?' she asked the assistant, thinking it was a sales gimmick.

'No, indeed not!' was the reply. 'But it would be a good idea.' It seems Jan was on an angel trail of synchronicity.

November 5

The angels in high places who minister to us,

Reflect God's smile, their faces are luminous.

ROBERT GILBERT WALSH

Guiding Light Insight

Let us honour those who have loved and cared for us, and give them the acknowledgement and recognition they deserve.

Daily Affirmation

Today, I accept love and I accept that love is all there is.

November 6

Divine Key

**We must all embrace the miracles of Nature and give
thanks to our planet and Mother Earth.**

Blessing

*May the Angel of Dawn illuminate my inner light
at the start of each day.*

November 7

Carole and Linda were great friends. Having recently lost her mother and moved to a new area, Carole was feeling very lost. Linda and her family were wonderful and helped Carole to settle in. Often she would stay overnight at Linda's house and, as Linda was an only child, the two girls thought of themselves as sisters. Sleeping in the attic room was good fun for them both. Linda's parents slept on a lower floor, as did Linda's grandmother, a sweet lady in her mid-nineties. Grandma was very frail and unwell at this point.

One night Carole woke in the early hours, to see Linda's grandmother standing beside her bed. Reasoning that the elderly lady might simply be saying goodnight, Carole snuggled down and went back to sleep. However, the next morning the girls discovered that Grandma had died during the night. As Carole talked about her visit she became aware that Grandma had been far to ill to leave her bed and that she could never have climbed the attic steps. She then realised that Grandma was in fact not saying 'goodnight', but 'goodbye'.

November 8

The golden moments in the stream of life rush past us, and we see nothing but sand; the angels come to visit us, and we only know them when they are gone.

GEORGE ELIOT

Guiding Light Insight

Let us forgive ourselves for judging our bodies and their potential.

Daily Affirmation

Today, I am willing to release my resentment and anger.

November 9

Divine Key

Meditate and awaken yourself with the possibilities
that exist within your chakra system and your brain
and nervous system.

Blessing

May the Angel of Silence embrace my
sacred space.

November 10

It was November when Eva's husband Trevor died, a bleak time of the year in which to cope with such a loss. Arrangements had to be made for the funeral, but Eva didn't know which reading to choose. A couple of days later, she received a card with a copy of the familiar poem by Henry Scott-Holland, which talks about the concept that the loved one is simply in another room. It felt exactly right, and so it was read out at Trevor's funeral.

Somehow, the family survived Christmas. On Boxing Day night, Eva went to bed with a collection of the new books she had been given as gifts. Before choosing a book to read, Eva asked her angels for a sign that Trevor was safe and in heaven. She then chose a book, which fell open on her lap at the very page containing the piece they had read at Trevor's funeral. Not only did Eva recognise this as a sign from the angels, but also it suddenly hit her that this was exactly how she thought of Trevor. For years he had suffered from multiple sclerosis and so was often in another room. The message could not have been clearer.

November 11

In love all his works have been done, and in this love he has made everything serve us; and in this love our life is everlasting. Our beginning was when we were made, but the love in which he made us never had beginning. In it we have our beginning.

LADY JULIAN OF NORWICH

Guiding Light Insight

Life is so extraordinary and magical when we operate from the high vibrating energy of 'I am love'.

Daily Affirmation

Today, I am making a difference simply because I exist.

November 12

Divine Key

Divine guidance is the key that will lead you out of
the darkness and towards illumination.

Blessing

*May the Angel of Daylight infuse my mind with
knowledge and banish all fear.*

November 13

The silver envelope fell onto the doormat and Lydia knew at once what it contained. Her closest friends were about to celebrate their Silver Wedding anniversary. When the pleasure of the invitation had settled, she was overcome with a sense of foreboding, for it would involve a long drive to Suffolk. A very nervous driver, Lydia was filled with fear. Cumbria to Suffolk felt like a trip halfway around the world!

One night before the journey, Lydia had a remarkable dream. In it, she drove along a motorway before turning into a side road, where she came across a pub with a distinctive sign. A small chapel with washed pink walls appeared, as did a ford with ducks waddling across it. The dream continued, until she arrived at her friend's house, which was also pink with a small fountain in the front garden.

'I really must be worried!' she thought, and as she set off she asked her angel to guide her safely. The journey was pretty straightforward until she turned off the motorway and she felt the beginnings of butterflies in her tummy. However, looking ahead she saw the pub with the unusual sign from her dream. Then a little further was the chapel, and so it continued until at last she was guided all the way to her friend's house, which was pink with a garden fountain!

November 14

Leonardo da Vinci attributed many of his inventions to dreams and wrote, 'Why does the eye see a thing more clearly in dreams than the imagination when awake?'

Guiding Light Insight

Change happens around us but not to us, for we are not mere things but living beings.

Daily Affirmation

Today, I choose to experience all acts of kindness.

November 15

Divine Key

Wherever we leave off in one moment, or in one life,
becomes the starting point of the next moment and
the experience of our next lives.

Blessing

May the Angel of Youth give perfect health and
energy to my body.

November 16

The television studio was busy. Gary had an appointment there and Glennyce was waiting for him. It was a hectic day in Hollywood and the excitement of the Academy Awards filled the air as they met up.

Chatting to a very elegant lady, Glennyce and Gary were not at all surprised to learn that she had been a model before working behind the camera. She explained that her career had ended the day that she was involved in a horrific car accident. Close to death in intensive care, she realised that her entire face had been seriously injured and that her modelling career was effectively over. Drifting up from her unconscious state, she became aware of a figure at the end of her bed. It was a large, full-blown angel! The angel smiled and held out her arms to her as once more she fell into a deep sleep. For several days, every time she regained consciousness, the angel was there. One day, it dawned on her that the angel was watching over her to keep her fighting spirit intact. She spoke to the angel and said, 'It will be fine, I will survive. You can go now!' Incredibly, the angel did just that and the attractive young woman recovered to enjoy a new life.

November 17

*You cannot be brave if you've only had wonderful
things happen to you.*

MARY TYLER MOORE

Guiding Light Insight

True happiness can only manifest with peace of
mind and a compassionate attitude.

Daily Affirmation

Today, I deserve love and affection.

November 18

Divine Key

To love yourself and to love others is truly the
ultimate task of a lifetime.

Blessing

May the Angel of Fertility permit love to reach

out from me to every person.

November 19

People who practise the art of reiki are clearly close to the angels. So many times we have heard stories of people who have experienced an acute awareness of a presence, angelic touch or even the sight of an angel whilst practising reiki.

Josie was treating a friend who was recovering from a serious operation. The relaxation and comfort of the session were clearly helping. At one point soon after the operation, Josie had believed her friend would not pull through and the atmosphere of the session was very emotional. Her eyes filled with tears and she channelled as much love as possible to her friend during the treatment.

Suddenly a shaft of light filled the room. Josie turned towards the window, thinking the sun had broken through the grey of that day. It was not the sun, but there in the centre of the beam stood an angel. It did not appear to have wings, but was clothed in a long white garment and radiated pure love. Josie had tapped into a very special angelic wavelength.

November 20

We can do no great things – only small things with great love.

MOTHER TERESA

Guiding Light Insight

Let us have a solid, positive attitude and know that everything will work out for the highest good.

Daily Affirmation

Today, I have the courage to be my best self in good times and bad.

November 21

Divine Key

Make time for yourself. Seize the weekend to get
back on track. Unplug and resist the urge to run
errands. For seven hours, turn off your phones, com-
puters, television and go out into nature. Love
yourself, your body and your whole being.

Blessing

*May the Angel of Perception always
light my way.*

November 22

A few days after holding an angel workshop Glennyce and her friend Diane met for coffee. Diane is a much appreciated workshop secretary as well as a close friend of Glennyce's. The business side of the day was now being sorted out. There were bills to pay and expenses to enter. With her usual efficiency, Diane took the receipts bag she kept exclusively for this purpose and spread its contents onto the floor.

The two friends discussed the fact that many people had asked for another similar day in future. Diane came up with a good idea: 'Why not extend the day and include more unusual forms of workshop activities?' she suggested. She and Glennyce had mutual friends who taught t'ai chi and Indian drumming, so the ideas flowed and they decided to hold an Angel Festival at Christmas.

Only half an hour later, after Diane had reached home, Glennyce received a phone call from her startled friend. Diane explained that she had been delving into the bag she had emptied out only a short time earlier and looking in her purse, when a white, fluffy feather fell to the ground! The two women concluded that the angels endorsed the idea she had put forward. They held the festival and it was quite wonderful!

November 23

Learn to listen,
Opportunity sometimes knocks very softly.

H. JACKSON BROWN JNR

Guiding Light Insight

Our supply is truly limitless and is directly associated with love. All life can be seen as love. This is truly the essence of what we are in the world.

Daily Affirmation

Today, I express love for life in all my ideas and experiences.

November 24

Divine Key

In order to experience a new beginning we need to acknowledge an ending.

Blessing

May the Angel of Universal Service transmit divine healing to me and those I love.

November 25

The Austrian biologist Paul Kammerer researched in depth the phenomenon we call synchronicity. His work reveals many fascinating facts, especially the occurrence of what he terms 'clustering'. This is when a chain of coincidences happen and the interesting fact is that the more notice we take of this, the more the coincidences keep coming. It is as if we need to 'plug in' to the spiritual wavelength that allows these wonderful coincidences to happen.

Beverley had just had her fortieth birthday and was standing at a crossroad in her life, when her life began to be transformed by magical moments of synchronicity. We feel her experiences are so inspiring that we have decided to feature them over the next few days. Hopefully, you too will feel inspired to ask your angels to help you into the wavelength that produces synchronicity.

November 26

*Some things arrive at their own mysterious hour,
on their own terms, and not yours, to be seized, or
relinquished forever.*

GAIL GODWIN

Guiding Light Insight

Positive visualisation can break the cycle of negative
thinking. It is the one tool that can be used to
change the way we think about ourselves. It can help
us to overcome adversity and negative thinking, and
it can help us believe in our talents and abilities.

Daily Affirmation

Today, I treat myself and others with kindness.

November 27

Divine Key

When the mind is cluttered and distracted it can have a damaging impact on the body. This manifests itself in stress, anxiety and related symptoms. It can also affect your mood and make an impression not only on your own energy field, but also those of others and the environment around you. Pay attention to your thought processes.

Blessing

May the Angel of Body Power heal all my ailments.

November 28

Beverley was in turmoil. She had no idea which direction her life should take next. So she did the only thing she could think of at this point, and that was to ask the angels for help.

Out of the blue, she received a phone call asking if she would like to take part in a weekend workshop in London at Regent's College. Beverley jumped at the chance, thus kick-starting her 'coincidence clustering'! Rather timid by nature, Beverley had rarely been to London before and had never travelled there by herself, so the prospect of going there now was especially daunting.

A beautiful, blonde young lady sat next to Beverley on the train. She asked where Beverley was going and when she replied Regent's College, the girl said, 'That's my destination too, so allow me to take you there.' Arriving at Waterloo Station in London, the girl bought Beverley her ticket and guided her onto the underground train. The relief for Beverley was wonderful and, on leaving the train, she walked along with the young woman, feeling very happy and excited. Glancing ahead, she could see the college come into view. Turning to her companion to thank her for her help, Beverley was amazed to find the lovely lady had simply vanished!

November 29

Fate keeps on happening.

ANITA LOOS

Guiding Light Insight

Lessons in life seem to come not only because we need them, but because we are receptive to them.

Daily Affirmation

Today, I open my body to a pure healing energy.

November 30

Divine Key

Whatever the limitations or beliefs are that we have
installed in our minds, we can effortlessly shed
them, regardless of how long or for what purpose we
previously held on to them.

Blessing

*May the Angel of Inner Healing bring wisdom
and unconditional love into my soul.*

December 1

That weekend in London coincidences happened frequently for Beverley. Although she lived in Bournemouth, her home town was in fact Cheltenham and she was amazed to find that two-thirds of people attending the workshop lived in Cheltenham.

At the end of the weekend, Beverley signed on at college for further studies, a brave step for her that she could never have taken without angelic help.

Her new studies eventually led to her making a job application. However, the interview required her to travel to another city. She would need to find some overnight accommodation, which became a worry as everywhere within her price range appeared to be booked. The last telephone number she tried included the digits 444, which is an 'angel number'. Well of course they had a vacant room and her accommodation problems were solved!

Landing the new job would be essential for Beverley and her family as they were facing a financial crisis and had to settle a large bill that they hadn't the means to pay. Crying miserably one night alone in their bedroom, Beverley asked the angels for help once more. The following day, a letter arrived about a pension scheme that her husband had been involved in fifteen years previously. Inside there was a cheque for exactly the amount needed to settle the outstanding bill!

December 2

Tears may be dried up, but the heart – never.

MARGUERITE DE VALOIS

Guiding Light Insight

Every moment is a new beginning. Live in this precious moment.

Daily Affirmation

Today, I let go of the past and live in the now.

December 3

Divine Key

Everything in life conforms to divine harmony. The
action of Divine right moves through you to create
perfect order and harmony in every aspect of your life.

Blessing

May the Angel of Childhood help me to create
right-minded decisions and perfect actions.

December 4

At ninety-two years of age, Edith was a strong, independent woman. Her neighbour Doreen was a kind and helpful soul who would take Edith to the supermarket once a week to buy her groceries. Apart from this, Edith was reluctant to ask for help from anyone.

One evening she received a telephone call from two very dear friends. They would be passing through the area briefly the following morning and asked Edith if they might call by for coffee. Edith was delighted and mortified at the same time. She had nothing in her cupboard to offer them to go with their coffee. In the past a lovely freshly baked cake would have awaited them, and now the lack of a cake or biscuits hurt Edith's pride and was a huge problem for her. Feeling stressed, she waited for their knock on the door.

Shortly before the friends were due to arrive, Doreen came calling. She handed Edith a large chocolate cake, saying she had just been to the church fair, and had picked up a treat for Edith! 'Doreen,' said Edith, 'you are an angel.'

December 5

Always be an angel-on-call for a friend.

ANONYMOUS

Guiding Light Insight

**Each one of us comes to this planet to express love;
it is the most wonderful and absolute purpose we
have in life.**

Daily Affirmation

Today, I am a beacon of light.

December 6

Divine Key

Change and awareness will be yours the moment you
put notions like 'hoping' and 'trying' to one side, and
actually start 'becoming'.

Blessing

May the Angel of Security bring me faith in
myself.

December 7

Every morning Norman would pass by the little café on his way to the bus stop. Sometimes, if he had time to spare, he popped in for a coffee. The owner and his wife were very fond of Norman and would cheerily wave to him and wish him good morning each day. Today it was a Friday morning, the busiest day of the week, and the café was full. When Norman walked past as usual on his way to work, several people waved to him and shouted, 'Good morning!' But inexplicably that day Norman did not respond.

During the following week, the café owner remarked to his wife that he had not seen Norman for several days and they wondered if maybe he was ill and resting at home. Two regular customers arrived and ordered their usual coffee and cake. 'Sad about Norman,' one of the men remarked.

'Is he seriously ill?' the café owner asked.

'Worse than that,' came the reply. 'He died suddenly in his sleep last Thursday.' He handed the owner the local paper, which confirmed the sad news. The owner and his wife exchanged shocked glances: that Friday morning, Norman must have been having one last look around to say goodbye, they decided.

December 8

Glories stream from heaven afar,

Heavenly host sings Allelujah!

JOSEPH MOHR

Guiding Light Insight

This particular lifetime represents an aspect of our eternal spiritual journey. We must not worry about comparing ourselves to others or getting it all right. Each moment and place is its own perfect experience.

Daily Affirmation

Today, I am newly born in every moment.

December 9

Divine Key

If you realise that the only things opposing your good
are your own self-imposed concepts of life, you can
begin to speak the truth in prayer calmly, quietly and
confidently. Give yourself the gift of being the real
you.

Blessing

*May the Angel of Ability activate my path
of service.*

December 10

We are rapidly approaching the darkest period of the year. It is a time when, for thousands of years, man has celebrated the winter solstice in order to bring light into the darkness. All the world's major religions celebrate light over darkness in the winter months. New traditions often overlay ancient beliefs and customs. We feel rejuvenated by the festivals of light that can be spiritually uplifting.

Hanukkah, the Jewish festival of light, involves the lighting of candles each night for eight nights, representing the time it took for the oil to reach the Temple after the destruction by the Assyrians. Only a tiny amount of oil was in the lamp, but miraculously it burned brightly until fresh supplies were brought. Diwali, the Hindu festival, also features lamps being lit. Christian countries celebrate the birth of Christ at this time of the year, and their celebrations also place the emphasis on light. Angels feature in all these religions and link us all with their wonderful light.

December 11

To me every hour of the light and dark is a
*   miracle,*
Every cubic inch of space is a miracle.

WALT WHITMAN

Guiding Light Insight

Since earliest times, the secret teachings of the
divine mysteries have been contained in the Torah.
The study of Kabbalah aims to understand the principles of cause and effect: that behind every effect
lies a motivating cause.

Daily Affirmation

Today, I understand the natural order of life and
I see the bigger picture.

December 12

Divine Key

Our relationships can take us to the threshold of our willingness to grow. When this happens, it is not necessarily an indication of whether we should stay in a relationship. It simply reveals that something deeper is taking place and that we must pay attention to what is going on.

Blessing

May the Angel of Empathy help me to discover my best self.

December 13

If anyone had asked Vicky what exactly was troubling her, she could not have articulated it. She was simply feeling the strain of juggling all the parts of her life. The needs of her family and her busy job were taking their toll, and she was extremely tired. Seeing Vicky's distress, a close friend offered her a few days alone in a cottage far away from the 'madding crowd'! Tears of gratitude sprang to her eyes as Vicky thanked her friend, recognising that this break was precisely what she had longed for.

Those two nights alone in beautiful surroundings were the best Christmas gift that Vicky had ever been given. Long walks in the crisp air and no clock-watching worked their magic and she felt herself unwind. Late at night, gazing into the clear sky, Vicky said, 'Thank you' to the higher force she felt was looking after her. At that point, a shooting star blazed across the night sky. Vicky interpreted that as saying, 'You're welcome!'

December 14

All round the circle of the sky I hear the spirit's voice.

NATIVE AMERICAN SAYING

Guiding Light Insight

Love is truth that comes from the heart, and when we are continually in love with life we vibrate according to that truth.

Daily Affirmation

Today, I share my knowledge and embrace new traditions.

December 15

Divine Key

The word 'mantra' comes from the root *manas*, which refers to the linear, thinking mind. *Tram* means 'to protect', 'to free', and 'to go across'. Thus, mantras are sonic formulae that can take us beyond, or through, the discursive faculties of the mind and connect our awareness to deep states of energy and consciousness.

Blessing

May the Angel of Hidden Power unite each living being.

December 16

It was the morning of the nativity play and the Sunday school children were getting into their costumes. The little church congregation was swollen by family and friends eagerly awaiting the performance. Everything was perfect, no one forgot their lines, and the singing from the little ones was quite beautiful. The child taking the part of Mary beamed at her mother and father in the congregation; the love in that tiny church was palpable.

At the back of the church, waiting to step forward to close the proceedings, stood the vicar with a tear in his eye. Suddenly, behind little Mary, he observed the light increase, glowing all around the child. The soft white light formed two wings which grew in size until they encompassed the entire group of children. As the vicar moved down the aisle, the light disappeared and he knew that, although the congregation had not witnessed the phenomenon, the angels were revelling in the love and spreading their light on that wonderful December morning.

December 17

How silently, how silently,
The wondrous gift is given!

BISHOP PHILLIPS BROOKS

Guiding Light Insight

A person with little love will often seek out powerful
positions in life without giving any thought as to
what they may have to do to get there. Such a person
may create the sort of success that brings back little
reward in terms of nurturing or love, because that
person offers little in this area themselves.

Daily Affirmation

Today, I accept awareness of my spiritual truth
and live joyously and fully.

December 18

Divine Key

Each day, be a little more compassionate, loving and
kind. Do this with your family, friends, co-workers,
neighbours and even strangers. Recognise that the
root that supports these actions is pure love.

Blessing

*May the Angel of Self-Image shower my soul
with the capacity to give and accept love.*

December 19

It was a bitterly cold night when Barbara drove to her sister's house to deliver Christmas gifts. Barbara would be away from home for the Christmas period, which she had mixed feelings about as she would miss her family. Maybe Barbara lost concentration at that moment … whatever the cause, she found her car sliding on the icy road and hitting a wall with force.

As she lay seriously ill in hospital that night, the medical staff delivered a gloomy prognosis. Slowly, however, she began to improve. Miraculously, only days after the accident, Barbara was able to chat with her family.

One morning the nurse who was attending her remarked on how well she was recovering. Barbara said that she felt that the beautiful music they had played to her must have helped. Puzzled, the nurse replied that no one had played music for her at any time.

'I was certain it came through the window from your office,' Barbara told them. The nurse pointed out that the window in question faced outside, and they were six stories up!

'It must have been the angels,' Barbara declared and, to her surprise, the nurse simply nodded in agreement.

December 20

Angels we have heard on high,

Sweetly singing o'er the plains,

And the mountains in reply

Echoing their joyous strains.

NINETEENTH-CENTURY HYMN

Guiding Light Insight

This very moment, we can reclaim our true identities
in the realm of eternal divine love. Each soul will
experience love in its unique way. Let us choose to
activate this presence of divine love in the sacred
moment of now.

Daily Affirmation

Today, I am a money magnet and create

financial abundance.

December 21

Divine Key

Find a way to make a contribution, whether it be
through using your talents to pursue meaningful
work, volunteering your time to help those in need,
or in some other way.

Blessing

*May the Angel of Detachment disconnect me
from all negativity.*

December 22

You may be familiar with the expression 'into everyone's life a little rain must fall' but sadly for Claudia, 'a little rain' had become a deluge! Living in England, far away from the sunshine of her native Columbia, the rain was literal and metaphorical. One night, when her problems appeared insurmountable and she was missing her family in Columbia dreadfully, she found herself in tears. Sitting in bed, she prayed for help and guidance. Instantly she became aware of the most beautiful, all-enveloping music. This, she realised, was heavenly music and, try as she might, Claudia still finds it almost impossible to describe.

What followed next will stay with Claudia for the rest of her life. Her room was filled with angels, all flawlessly beautiful with almost childlike faces in their innocence, and gracefully dancing. They were playing many musical instruments including harps as they danced. Perhaps the most amazing feature of this vision was the fact that the angels were wearing long, heavy medieval-type gowns that appeared to be made from rich hues of velvet. It was a truly awesome event. To this day Claudia can recall the beautiful music in her head as a lifelong reminder of her night with the angels.

December 23

The garments of the angels correspond to their intelligence. The garments of some glitter as with flame and those of others are resplendent as with light, others are of various colours, and some white and opaque.

EMANUEL SWEDENBORG

Guiding Light Insight

When we are in touch with the angelic kingdom, we can't help but be connected to our own soul.

Daily Affirmation

Today, I am vibrant, passionate and
full of vitality.

December 24

Divine Key

The angelic life is around you throughout your day.
Talk to your angels and listen for their answers. You
may hear words or receive impressions from them.
Or perhaps the answers will come to you
instantaneously.

Blessing

*May the Angel of Esoteric Philosophy radiate
through my whole being, focusing me in who I
am right here and now.*

December 25

At just six months old, Sharna was seriously ill with pneumonia. Her condition deteriorated so quickly that the doctors had warned her mother, Maggi, that the chances of her surviving were pretty slim. Day and night, Maggi sat in the hospital by her daughter's bedside, dozing from time to time in a comfy chair.

Trying hard to pray in the early hours, Maggi simply began to talk to God as if to a friend. She fell asleep, but woke with a start and thought she could smell smoke. Her first reaction was that the curtains were on fire. Shouting for help, she ran to find the nurses who quickly returned with Maggi to the little girl's bedside. There was no smoke but this time Maggi recognised the smell. Early in her life she had attended church devotions and she was sure that this was the familiar fragrance of frankincense!

Slowly Sharna improved and the following morning the doctors were delighted with her progress. She became known as the miracle baby. Sharna recovered from the pneumonia but sadly only lived to the age of twelve. However, she profoundly influenced her mother's life and the lives of all who came into contact with her.

December 26

The angels descended, trailing their wonderful
incense to comfort and heal.

MARY TRENCHER

Guiding Light Insight

There is something amazing for everyone to
experience in this life. If we can live without any
limitations we can create magnificent miracles.

Daily Affirmation

Today, I am surrounded by love and light.

December 27

Divine Key

When we begin to trust life we will find that magic
will enter our lives and we will begin to see the alignment of everything and everyone change. Ultimately,
love will appear. This is the divine key of life: love is
all there is.

Blessing

May the Angel of All Living Things bring

Oneness into my life.

December 28

Meditation on Trust

Step 1: Assume a comfortable position. Close your eyes and just let go. For the next few moments, there is nothing else to do, nowhere else to go, but to be here, now.

Step 2: Take a deep breath and when you have filled your lungs, hold it. At the same time, with your eyelids closed, look up at the top of your head. Hold the eye position and your breath for a few seconds only. Then just slowly let them relax and, as you do, feel yourself relaxing, floating.

Step 3: Feel your body relaxing as you continue to breathe slowly and deeply. Breathing in … and breathing out … Release any tension … Allowing passing thoughts to drift away … Feel the golden energy of the Earth coming in through the soles of your feet, moving through your entire body … Feel how this golden energy grounds you, creating a space of safety … creating a connection to all that is. Now feel energetic light from the loving source of the Universe come down through the top of your head, filling your entire body … Feel the perfection of this moment … Take a deep breath. Affirm your trust in life and the Universe.

December 29

Divine Key

Meditation is a practice that will help you to clean up the clutter in your mind and open a channel of communication with your angels. While praying you talk to God or your angels. When meditating you must listen to messages they will give to you.

Blessing

May the Angel of Universal Love and Light touch, bless, protect and love everyone and everything.

December 30

There comes a time in most of our lives when we wonder why on earth we are doing our job. Despite all our best efforts negative feedback may leave us feeling undervalued and low in spirits. This was exactly how Gillian was feeling as she left home one morning, but she was relieved to be attending a talk that she hoped might lift her spirits. The talk was going to be about musical instruments and their heavenly counterparts.

The atmosphere in the lecture room was wonderful and very loving. The speaker's wife was gazing upon him with pride and affection. As Gillian watched the dynamics between the two, something amazing happened.

Directly behind the speaker's wife, a figure appeared and it became obvious that this was an angel. Tall, with wings reaching to waist level, this heavenly being radiated a silver glow. A silver haze surrounded his head and his garments also shone silver. His hair particularly had a silver sheen, as did his face, body and hands. It was an awesome sight and Gillian felt her heart sing. All feelings of sadness lifted and, as the figure disappeared, Gillian felt sensations of pure joy. It was as if the angel had responded to the love in the room and the need in Gillian for strength and comfort at that point in her life.

December 31

Where love abounds,
The angels hover overhead.

ANONYMOUS

Guiding Light Insight

Let us live life as if each moment is our last.

Daily Affirmation

Today, I am free to create whatever I desire. I love myself, I love life and I love all others! I am love!

Epilogue

We have arrived at the end of the year and here we stand on the threshold of a new twelve-month cycle, with all its unknown quantities. We sincerely hope the daily readings have been an inspiration and guided you through a dark day or two. You may wish to repeat the year's readings, or simply dip into the book whenever the spirit moves you.

We truly appreciate the contributions of the many people who willingly allowed us to include their very personal stories. They illustrate that the angels comfort and help us all, no matter what our walk of life, age or gender. This being the case, they will certainly help you too.

Remember you do not have to join an organisation, commit yourself to meetings, or study, to work with the angels. Angels represent a personal, one-to-one form of spirituality. All you have to do is to believe in them and trust – the angels will do the rest.

Begin your new year in the certain knowledge that help is at hand. Ask your angels to guide you through the coming seasons. If we all ask together we could truly make the coming year an *Annus Angelicus*!

Acknowledgements

We wish to thank the following very special people. Their support and encouragement have made the writing of this book such a joy:

Judith Kendra, Sue Lascelles, Sarah Bennie, Caroline Newbury, David Parrish, Emma Harrow, Ed Griffiths, Barbara Moulton, Evelyn M. Dalton, Frank H. Smith, Fern Britton, Philip Scofield, Ross Eckersley, Rachel Eckersley, Ed Potten, Gillian Smith, Michael Smith, Janice O'Gara, Valerie Bagarozzi, August Bagarozzi, Amanda Malloy, Terry Malloy, Leeza Gibbons, Anne Taylor, Cheryl Murphy, Vivien Gibson, Bryan Craig, Rebekah Paltrow, Cheryl Welch, Christopher Watt, Patty Q, Cira De La Cruz, Fiona Harrold, Kelly Wald, Jane Gibson of Brightlife, Pam Beldan, Jason Kinrade, Beverley Aldritt, Marylyn Brown, Margi Blackmore, Wendy Price, Carolyn Burdet, Doriana Mazola, Sante Losio, Kenny Feuerman, Andreas Kurtz, Iris Loesel, Ute Ville, Patricia McDonough, Amelia Kinkade, Liza Sullivan, Sherry Daech, Patricia Fleming, Christine Miller, Lois Weinstock, Thomas C. Achille and Cindy Schneider.

We now thank all those wonderful people who so kindly allowed us to include their very personal stories:

John and Mary Abbis, Patsy Allan, Madeline Allen-Holmes, Isabel Asher, Anne Bailey, Sue Barbosa, Sharon Botchway, Kath

Braden, Kath Burns, Cynthia Chamness, Janice Alison Chilton Bickerdike, Shirley Clarke, Debs Connell, Catherine Coverdale, Craig Crompton, Roy and Pam Cuthbert, Carol Dickson, Pat Geldard, Revd Gillian Gordon, Audrey Greenberg, Jonathan Greenberg, Beverley Gregory, Jane Hammond, Louise Hanratty, Revd John Harley, Mark Hughes, Maggi Kissane, Olga Kouapobou, Brenda Law, Amanda Lloyd, Lisa Mclaren, Diane Marsh, Myrna Michelle, Marina Moss, Padma O'Gara, Marie Pandolfo, Helen Parker, Tracy Pattin, Annie Perry, Julie Preston, Sheila Rodford, LesleyRoss, Margaret Ross, Barbara Ruft, Pam Shaw, Marie Strahan, Alice Tattersall, Carole Thaw, Jean Thornton, Nicola Walker, Aksi William, Eva Winstanley, Trevor Winstanley, Greta, Joanna and Daniel Woolf, and Stella, Megan, Fiona, Claudia and Ellen.